THE
CONQUEST
OF
CHILE

Pedro de Valdivia · Fran.co de Villagra · G.mo Alderete Adelantado

THE CONQUEST OF CHILE

BY H. R. S. POCOCK

STEIN AND DAY/*Publishers*/New York

Copyright © 1967 H. R. S. Pocock
Library of Congress Catalog Card No. 67-25618
All rights reserved
Designed by David Miller
Printed in the United States of America
Stein and Day/*Publishers*/7 East 48 Street, New York, N.Y. 10017

Preface

My book was, I think, first conceived in the nitrate *pampas* of the Atacama desert. My job was the distribution of petroleum, and some of my first years at it were spent in the north of Chile. In what was then an up-to-date Ford motorcar, I would drive for hours at a time through the desert without seeing anything but the whitened bones of some long dead mule, a derelict nitrate *Oficina* or two, and a constantly receding mirage. The sharp cold at night and the blazing heat of the midday sun supplied the only contrasts in these strangely fascinating wastes, though variety was sometimes provided in the form of a small whirlwind, which would spring up from nowhere and liberally pepper the car with sand and pebbles.

It was heavy going even in a motorcar on tolerable tracks which permitted speeds of up to fifty miles an hour and with the knowledge that the end of the journey meant comfortable quarters and a good meal. It was impossible not to speculate on how the original *Conquistadores* had ever managed, on horse and on foot, to penetrate this endless barren waste and so reach down to the green loveliness in which they finally settled.

Speculation led to the quest for information. I soon discovered that, with the exception of Cunninghame Graham's

Pedro de Valdivia, there was nothing available on the subject in my own language. Gradually I started perusing the Spanish accounts and finally found myself delving fascinatedly into the masses of original documents collected by José Toribio Medina from the *Archivos de Indias* in Spain. And so one day it had to occur to me that, as no account of what I wanted existed in English, I should have to try to write one for myself.

For the main account, I have been guided by the first volume of Francisco Encina's *Historia de Chile* and Monseñor Crescente Errazuriz's *Pedro de Valdivia.* I am indebted to Ricardo Latcham's *Prehistoria Chilena* and again to Francisco Encina for most of the material in the Appendix on the problem of the Araucanians.

The solid contemporary sources used have been Pedro de Valdivia's letters to Charles V and others, the Minutes of the Santiago Municipality, and the histories written by Gongora Marmolejo and Mariño de Lobera. These have been filled in with the evidence collected and published in thirty volumes by José Toribio Medina, already referred to above, in his *Documentos Inéditos para la historia de Chile.*

Finally I should like to record my gratitude to Reginald Doublet for his early encouragement: to John Shenton for his helpful comments on the first draft: and to the late Norman Chambers for the occasional use of his riverside bungalow near Tucapel, where Pedro de Valdivia met his death. This last combination of atmosphere with what must be some of the best wet-fly trout fishing in the world provides unforgettable memories.

Les Nièmes
August, 1966

Table
of
Contents

Maps
and
Illustrations

1

Events
Leading up
to the
Conquest

This is to some extent just the story of the opening rounds of a fight, of a fight by a small but incomparably stouthearted people for its liberty, a fight which has earned, and may one day be accorded, a very special chapter of its own in man's history.

For more than three hundred years the members of this primitive race, probably never numbering as many as 400,000 individuals, stubbornly maintained their independence in the face of all that could be brought against them by their European aggressors. While the *Picunches,* their northern neighbours, and the *Huilliches* to the south of them (see map) succumbed almost at the first contact, the Araucanians successfully defended a solid strip of territory running right across the middle of Chile from mountain to ocean, dividing it into two separate halves. Only when their numbers had been pitifully thinned, their blood ruthlessly drained by the combined ravages of disease and ten generations of warfare, was it possible to impose permanent terms of settlement upon them. The fight came to an end barely eighty years ago. Its primary and unlikely cause had been the quest for a sea route from western Europe to India.

Toward the end of the fifteenth century, the Turks had made themselves masters of western Asia, and were attacking and destroying the caravans which made the land journey from western Europe to India. This journey was sufficiently difficult and costly in any circumstances, only to be repaid by the fabulous prices which were obtained for the spices and precious stones brought back by the adventurous traders. The cutting of the land route by the Turks brought this lucrative business to an end, thereby creating a sharp spur to maritime enterprise and the most powerful of motives for the opening up of an alternative route by sea.

Portugal took the lead in these designs, selecting the obvious southern direction down the west coast of Africa, with the object of finally sailing round the extremity of that continent and so eastward into the Indian Ocean. Year by year her seamen crept farther down the African coast, at the cost of many failures and disasters, until finally in 1488 Bartolomeu Diaz reached the Cape of Good Hope. Nine years later Vasco da Gama completed the route right round the shores of the African continent and reached India.

Meanwhile Christopher Columbus had finally persuaded the Spanish monarchs to allow him to test a revolutionary idea, and to attempt to reach India by sailing not eastward but westward. He died without being in the least aware of what it was that he had really found during his four famous voyages.

Many adventurers continued to follow in the western footsteps of Columbus, believing, as he had, that they were exploring the outskirts of India. Two men were principally responsible for giving the lie to this belief, Amerigo Vespucio and Nuñez de Balboa. From the time the latter had made an expedition across the isthmus of Panama and discovered the vastness of the Pacific Ocean,[1] there could be no doubt that India had not yet been reached by the Western route, but that instead a great new continent now barred the way.

The discovery of the new continent was viewed with small satisfaction in Spain. She had now been left very far behind in the race for the riches of India and was prevented by a special circumstance from retracing her steps and following the Portuguese along the now well-opened Eastern route. In those days the Catholic countries of Europe regarded all lands inhabited by barbarians and infidels as belonging exclusively to the Pope. The Portuguese had obtained a concession from one holder of the office to exploit all the countries which they might discover in their voyages to the East. The Spaniards in their turn, after the first discoveries of Columbus, had sought and obtained from a later Pope a similar concession in the West. As a result they now found themselves barred from eastern expansion, since this Pope, in order to avoid subsequent causes of troubles between the two peoples, had drawn an imaginary dividing line from pole to pole, cutting down across the Atlantic Ocean 370 leagues west of the Azores. The Spaniards could only become masters of the lands west of this line, everything to the east of it being the special preserve of the Portuguese. There was nothing for it, therefore, but to discover a means of sailing round or through what was regarded as an unwanted barrier to their legitimate ambitions in India, and to this end the Spaniards devoted their energies.

The first expedition made in a southerly direction under Juan Diaz de Solis was a failure. After reaching the South American coast, he sailed south to the River Plate, which he took to be a strait leading through to the Pacific. He therefore sailed up the estuary and, landing on an island, was attacked by the inhabitants and killed with the rest of his party. The survivors of the expedition returned to Spain to report the disaster.

Four years later, the first boat to sail round the world set out from Sanlúcar. It was one of a fleet of five ships under the command of Magellan, who discovered and sailed through the Straits that now bear his name.

In crossing the Pacific he lost the greater part of his crews to bad weather and hunger before reaching the Philippines. Here he himself met his death at the hands of the natives. In the tiny *Victoria,* the only ship left of the original five, Sebastian del Cano sailed onward past the much desired India and, after completing the long journey round the continent of Africa, finally brought his stout little vessel into the port of Sanlúcar, whence she had departed on her great adventure just three years before.

Meanwhile the new continent was attracting adventurers on its own account, and colonization was actively in progress on the shores of the Caribbean from Mexico to Venezuela. Exploration had so far been confined to the eastern side of the continent, though there were persistent rumors regarding the existence of countries to the west, countries literally teeming with the gold which was the principal attraction of the Spanish emigrants.

As we have seen, Nuñez de Balboa was the first of the explorers to reach the far shores of the continent, after crossing the Isthmus of Panama. Picturesquely rushing into the waters of this new ocean, fully armed, he claimed it and all that it contained for the king of Castille. Little did he comprehend, says Prescott, the full import of his magnificent vaunt.

Balboa proceeded to push his discoveries some twenty

leagues south of the Gulf of St. Michael, in quest of the land of the Incas. He was doomed, however, to fall a victim of the jealousy of the governor under whom he served, Don Pedro Arias de Avila, more usually referred to as Pedrarias, before his ambitious projects could be brought to a successful conclusion.

Pedrarias was by no means insensible to the advantages accruing from Balboa's discoveries and in 1519 transferred his capital from Darién to the ancient site of Panama, now a favorite haunt for tourists, which lies to the east of the present city of that name..The principal object was still the discovery of a maritime passage from ocean to ocean, and exploration for a year or two was directed northward, or rather westward, in the hope of finding a strait through the comparatively narrow isthmus. A steady territorial advance was made until the forces of Pedrarias made contact in Honduras with the warriors of Cortés, who were on their way South after completing the conquest of Mexico. The meeting put an end to all hope of finding a strait in this direction.

From this point onward, exploration in a southerly direction from Panama began to be taken seriously in hand. An expedition in 1522 under Pascual de Andagoya made no progress beyond the limits of Balboa's discoveries, and had to be abandoned owing to the ill health of its leader. Not long afterward, however, the quest was taken up by the two individuals who were destined to share the glory of the final discovery and conquest of the Empire of the Incas, after such a display of endurance and audacity as has rarely been equaled.

Francisco Pizarro, the leader of the enterprise, belongs only to the history of Peru. His companion, however, Diego de Almagro, was to lead the first Spanish expedition into Chile and so requires more particular description.

13

He was born illegitimately about the year 1480 in the village of Almagro in Etremadura. His mother, Elvira Gutierrez, defrauded in her hope of marrying his father, a certain Juan de Montenegro, cupbearer to the Master of Calatrava, was deprived also of her child Diego, who, for the sake of the family honor, was sent secretly to Bolaños and entrusted to the care of a certain Sancha Lopez de Peral. Before he was five years old, the child was claimed by his father, who, however, died shortly afterward, leaving him in the charge of Hernan Gutierrez, his mother's brother.

Almagro's headstrong character brought frequent and severe punishment upon himself at the hands of Gutierrez, and he finally ran away from his uncle's home when fourteen or fifteen years old. While leading the life of a vagrant, he one day approached his mother, now married to one Zellinos in Ciudad Real, and asked for a piece of bread. "Take this, son," answered his mother, giving him some bread and a sum of money, "take this and do not hurt me more. Go from me, and may God aid you in your venture."[2] This was the last heard of Almagro by his family until, more than forty years later, they were astonished to learn that the famous and immensely wealthy *Adelantado* and Governor for His Majesty of the province of New Toledo was no other than the vagrant urchin who years gone by had been dismissed by his mother with a crust of bread. Juan de Espinoza, his servant, brought the sensational tidings while on a visit to Spain for the principal purpose of arranging a marriage for Almagro's son, Diego de Almagro the younger.

Almagro's career on the new continent began in 1514, when he set out for Panama under Pedrarias. Here he became acquainted with Francisco Pizarro and began that curious friendship which was to end so disastrously to himself. Like Pizarro, he was completely illiterate, not knowing even how to sign his own name. Yet he was intelligent, possessed great initiative and energy, and was generous to a fault. How often in the story of his partnership, and finally of his struggle, with the more crafty Pizarro can be discerned all the simple human characteristics of a noble and warmhearted disposition, characteristics which, while endearing him to his followers, finally put him at the mercy of his more cold-blooded antagonist. With all his faults of birth, manners, and education, Diego de Almagro stands out strikingly as one of the more likable characters in the story of Latin American conquest.

The two friends, having resolved upon their great undertaking, made good their lack of the necessary funds through the medium of a third partner, Hernando de Luque, who represented the Licentiate Gaspar de Espinosa, and after obtaining Governor Pedrarias' consent, rapidly carried through their preparations.

Their first inconclusive expedition as far as Punta Quemada, though it seems to have exasperated Pedrarias, simply served to convince the three partners of the truth lying behind the rumors of a flourishing empire farther south and led them to the drawing up and signing, Pizarro and Almagro by proxy, of the famous document by which "three obscure individuals coolly carved out and partitioned among themselves an empire of whose extent, power, and resources, of whose situation, of whose existence even, they had no sure or precise knowledge" (Prescott). Pedrarias, meanwhile, had been prevailed upon to give his grudging consent to a further attempt being made, though stipulating that his own share should now be bought out by payment of the sum of one thousand *pesos de oro*. By this act of meanness, entirely in keeping with his character, Pedrarias most fittingly deprived himself of a major share in the vast spoil of the Incas.

The dramatic success of the two succeeding expeditions, which must finally have exceeded the wildest dreams of the most optimistic of the adventurers who took part in them, is too well-known to require further description, nor is it to our present purpose. We are concerned only with those later stages which affected the relations between Pizarro and Almagro, and finally led to the latter's undertaking his expedition to Chile.

After the division of the enormous booty which had been collected from all parts of Peru by the Inca Atahualpa, for the payment of a ransom which he was never accorded, Hernando Pizarro, Francisco's elder brother, was selected to be the bearer of the great news, as well as of the Royal Fifth of the treasure, to Spain. It was also part of his mission to claim suitable rewards and honors for the leaders of the successful expedition. Almagro was careful on this occasion to see that his own merits were properly recognized, and sent independent representatives for this purpose to the Spanish court.

It was a messenger sent by Almagro's friends who first returned to Peru with news of the results of the mission. He bore the tidings of Almagro's elevation to the rank of Governor, for the King, of the Province of New Toledo. This made Almagro the titular equal of Pizarro and gave him complete independence from his old associate. The limits of New Toledo were two hundred Spanish leagues of territory, measured from the southern boundary of Pizarro's province of New Castille.

The news reached Almagro just after he had assumed, by Pizarro's appointment, the governorship of the city of Cuzco. He had taken it over from Pizarro's brothers, Juan and

Gonzalo. Greatly elated by the tidings from his friends in Spain, he let it be known that he now governed Cuzco quite independently of any appointment from Pizarro, since the city fell within the limits of his own province of New Toledo. Juan and Gonzalo Pizarro lost no time in informing Francisco of this disagreeable and indeed alarming turn of events.

Francisco Pizarro, as yet unaware that his own province of New Castille had been lengthened seventy leagues southward, thus bringing Cuzco within its borders, suspected that Almagro's claims might be true. He nevertheless sent word to Almagro requesting him temporarily to return the control of the city to his brothers until the official documents of appointment should arrive from Spain, alleging that it would be unseemly for Almagro to receive them when already enjoying the privileges they conferred. Almagro refused, and when the spirits of the two factions in Cuzco were reaching boiling point, Pizarro himself arrived upon the scene.

Once again the two partners were able to patch up their differences, owing to the coolness of Pizarro on the one hand and the warmhearted, if impetuous, temperament of Almagro on the other. The knowledge of the gold tribute which came from Chile each year, the picture of Chilean prosperity which was deliberately painted for him by the Peruvian Indians who were secretly planning rebellion and wished to be rid of as many Spaniards as possible, and finally the appeals of numbers of the Spanish soldiery who flatteringly looked to him to lead them to new and rich discoveries, all conspired to inflame Almagro's imagination and induce him to fall in with Pizarro's proposals. An agreement was reached by which Almagro should lead an expedition to Chile, a great deal of whose present extent lay within the bounds of his new province, leaving the question of Cuzco to be settled on purely technical grounds and in the light of whatever might develop out of the Chilean enterprise. If Almagro found good country, he was to settle his new province 130 leagues south of Cuzco. If, however, he were dissatisfied, he could return and resume his full share of the rewards of Peru. A formal contract renewing the partnership was signed on June 12, 1535. Its terms, designed to prolong the life of the association of the two men, merely succeeded in making explicit the death of their friendship. Each, resentful and afraid of the other, was attempting by the futile expedient of a written document to defend himself from an overt or underhand attack. What these former friends so solemnly signed on that June day, during Mass and "after the saying of the Lord's prayer," was not so much an agreement as a negation of the very possibility of their ever agreeing again.

In such an atmosphere, Almagro raised his banner for the South and so set in motion the train of events which, within a few months, would bring Spaniard and Araucanian face to face for the first time.

2

Expedition
of
Diego de Almagro

Almagro's first task was to secure his line of advance. A choice of two roads was open to him.

When the Incas first invaded Chile, they had taken the most direct route across her present northern border and down along the western slopes of the Andes. It had the considerable disadvantage of making necessary the crossing of that long stretch of desert which, had the Spaniards known it, contained Chile's principal wealth, not indeed the gold which these pioneers so eagerly sought, but the far more profitable mineral known to their descendants as nitrate of soda. As ignorant of this treasure as the Spaniards, the Incas had subsequently developed a more easterly route through what is now Bolivia and the northern part of the Argentine Republic. This road emerged at one point into the Copiapó valley by way of the San Francisco pass across the Andes and farther south into the Aconcagua valley by way of the Uspallata pass, and came to be normally employed as their regular means of communication.

After consultation with the Inca Manco, who, as the legitimate son of Huaina Capac, was the rightful heir to the throne and had actually been installed upon it with consid-

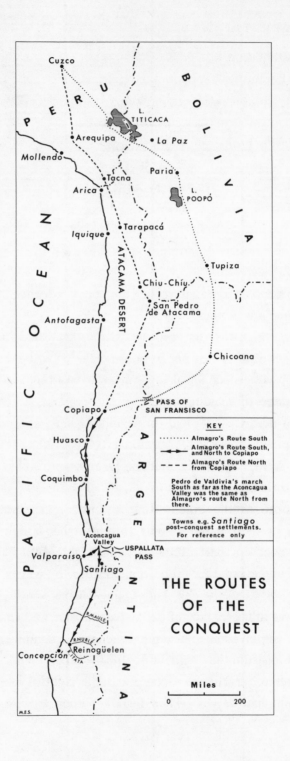

THE ROUTES
OF THE
CONQUEST

PERU

BOLIVIA

PACIFIC OCEAN

ARGENTINA

ATACAMA DESERT

Cuzco

L. TITICACA

Arequipa

La Paz

Mollendo

Paria

Tacna

L. POOPÓ

Arica

Iquique

Tarapacá

Tupiza

Chiu-Chiu

San Pedro
de Atacama

Antofagasta

Chicoana

PASS OF
SAN FRANSISCO

Copiapo

Huasco

Coquimbo

Aconcagua
Valley

USPALLATA
PASS

Valparaíso

Santiago

R. MAULE

R. NUBLE

ÑATA

Reinogüelen

Concepción

KEY

.... Almagro's Route South

⟵————⟶ Almagro's Route South,
and North to Copiapo

– – – – Almagro's Route North
from Copiapo

Pedro de Valdivia's march
South as far as the Aconcagua
Valley was the same as
Almagro's route North from
there.

Towns e.g. *Santiago*
post-conquest settlements.
For reference only

Miles

0   200

M.E.S.

erable ostentation by Pizarro, Almagro decided on the second of the alternatives. Though the Spanish conquest had weakened the Inca grip on the outlying posts of the Empire, the basic organization still remained in being under the nominal control of the puppet Emperor. It was not difficult for Almagro to avail himself of such advantages as this state of affairs afforded.

The immediate and willing assistance given by Manco, in reponse to the Spaniard's appeal, has sometimes been attributed to a desire to ingratiate himself with his masters in the hope that they would eventually help him to the reality as well as to the semblance of power. It is far more probable, however, in the light of subsequent events, and indeed in that of the character of Manco himself, that he was already plotting rebellion and welcomed the opportunity of thus easily ridding Peru of so substantial a proportion of the invaders. The actions of his emissaries, sent ahead of Almagro to smooth his passage, can in fact hardly be interpreted in any other manner.

These emissaries so spontaneously placed at Almagro's disposal were no less personages than prince Paullo Tupac, Manco's brother, and Villac Umu, the High Priest of all the Incas, whose combined knowledge and influence could clearly be of the greatest usefulness not only in determining the most advantageous methods of organizing each section of the journey, but even more importantly in ensuring the friendly assistance of the natives through whose territory the Spaniards would have to pass.

From the preliminary knowledge which Almagro was able to obtain regarding the general nature of the country which lay ahead of him, he judged it wiser for his force to proceed south in several separate units. To prepare the way, he first sent forward three Spaniards to accompany, and no doubt to keep an eye upon, Paullo Tupac and Villac Umu, with instructions to await his own arrival in Tupiza, a town situated some two hundred leagues from Cuzco. He next sent to Lima his captains Ruy Diaz and Juan de Herrada with a commission to raise a force there, and at the same time to fit out two or three vessels with the necessary stores and replenishments and so supplement by this easier means of transport the amount of supplies which it was possible to carry overland. Almagro himself devoted his energies to raising the main force in Cuzco and was soon in a position to send forward a hundred men under Juan Saavedra, who had orders to halt at Pária, 130 leagues on the road south, and there to gather together as much as possible in the way of supplies with which to provision the whole force on the next stage of the journey. Saavedra carried out his instructions with the greatest efficiency, and was successful also in being able to incorporate under his command a further fifty recruits. These men had formed the greater part of a company of sixty who were in the territory under the leadership of Gabriel de Rojas. Rojas, who held a commission from Pizarro, avoided the encounter for fear of arrest and returned with his remaining ten companions to Peru. This well-authenticated but little noticed incident is of considerable interest from the striking evidence it affords, not merely of the bitterness, but of the widespread notoriety of the relations existing between Pizarro and Almagro.

Almagro set out from Cuzco on July 3, 1535, with a following of about fifty Spaniards. He left Rodrigo de Orgoñez in Cuzco to complete the organization of the remaining forces, which were to follow at the earliest moment. Several of the contemporary accounts ascribe Almagro's failure to complete his preparations in Cuzco to the sudden realization that, with the departure of Saavedra's men, he was practically at Pizarro's mercy. It is even stated that his departure was in fact precipitated by the fear of summary arrest. Herrera adds to this story the twist that it was Pizarro himself who had his supposed intention indirectly conveyed to Almagro in order to ensure no further delay in his rival's departure. Whatever the truth or otherwise of these accounts, they assuredly provide nothing that would indicate any attempt at reconciliation between the former friends.

After a short halt in the village of Moira, some four leagues south of Cuzco, Almagro pushed forward rapidly and, proceeding by way of the west bank of Lake Titicaca, in due course reached Pária, where Saavedra was awaiting him. Further time was spent in making preparations in this rich district, which was to supply the expedition with grain and clothing and the animals which were to serve on the journey ahead, first as beasts of burden and finally for meat. Here also were obtained the large numbers of natives who were to act as the servants and porters of the Spanish adventurers.

At the end of a month, all was in readiness, and Almagro lost no further time before continuing the march. After passing Lake Poopó, he traversed the dry lands and the hilly regions beyond in good order, and finally reached Tupiza in October.

Here he was welcomed by Paullo Tupac and Villac Umu. There was no sign, however, of the three Spaniards who had accompanied the Inca nobles thus far. It soon appeared that in direct disobedience to Almagro's instructions, the three soldiers had decided to go forward alone and discover Chile for themselves, a feat which they were destined to accomplish at the cost of their lives. Of far greater interest, however, to

Almagro's followers than the meeting with the two Incas or the news regarding their three insubordinate companions was the gift which Paullo Tupac had prepared, consisting of all the gold which it had been possible to collect from the natives during his journey. In addition he had intercepted the messenger who was on his way north with the gold tribute from Chile, and had added this also to the welcome treasure. Herrera valued the total worth at about 90,000 *Castellanos*,[1] a figure which Mariño de Lobera more than doubles at 200,000. "And it was a sight to see," adds the latter, "the satisfaction with which the soldiers all hastened to question the messenger from Chile, each one by himself and for as long a time as he could, regarding the richness of the country; and the answers they obtained were so much to their taste, with the great weight of gold which the Indian promised, that he made them keener to move than a horse pricked by a spur." The sight of two nuggets, one weighing fourteen pounds and the other eleven, did nothing to diminish the enthusiasm.

If Almagro was now more fully aware of the difficulties which lay ahead of him, the knowledge in no way affected his determination to proceed. Even the news of the arrival in Peru of the Bishop of Panama, Thomas de Berlanga, specially commissioned to settle in the King's name the dispute over the exact borderline between New Castille and New Toledo, did nothing to shake his purpose of personally settling once and for all the question of Chile's merits. He continued to make careful preparations for the further advance during the whole of the two months which had to be spent in Tupiza until the grain there had ripened. Although no iron was available, and copper had, perforce, to be used for the purpose, all the horses were reshod in this interval.

At the turn of the year the march was resumed. Its character, however, quickly changed. During the stay in Tupiza, Villac Umu had suddenly decamped with the whole of his personal following, and there is very little doubt that his purpose, now that the golden bait had done its work, was to be back in Peru in time for the Indian rebellion, using his return journey to incite the natives now in Almagro's rear to rise against their oppressors and so cut off all mutual communication between Cuzco and the expedition. Nor was it only behind the Spaniards that this influence was being exerted. In front they began to find fierce opposition. Stragglers were quickly pounced upon and done to death by groups of Indians whom, however, the Spaniards were unable to bring to a pitched battle in which the outrages might be fittingly avenged. In a more than ordinarily elaborate attempt to come to grips with these foes, Almagro almost lost his life near the village of Chicoana.

On this occasion, after concealing his forces in suitable country, he deliberately sent out into the open his friendly Indian auxiliaries to act as bait. As he had planned, the enemy soon began to expose themselves in the excitement of seeing so easy a prey. The Spaniards had orders to await Almagro's command before breaking cover. Unfortunately, the strain proved too great for one of the hidden cavalrymen, who charged forward before the victims were properly in the trap. If not near enough to be cut to pieces, however, the natives were quite sufficiently far from cover to be chased, and in this Almagro himself took the lead. After spearing two of the hindmost of his intended victims, he was suddenly confronted by a third, who stopped and turned to shoot an arrow. So truly was this aimed that it killed Almagro's horse instantly, the beast pinning its rider beneath it in its fall. Juan Martin de Caceres was up only just in time to get his leader away in safety.[2]

After waiting in Chicoana long enough for the last of the snow to melt in the Andine passes, Almagro set his face toward the mountain range. He had now been joined by Noguera de Ulloa, who with a further fifty men had followed him all the way down from Cuzco, and it was at the head of a total of approximately 250 Spaniards that he reached the opening of the pass of San Francisco at the end of March.

All contemporary accounts are unanimous in stressing the hardships imposed by this crossing. After weeks of marching and fighting, poorly clothed and worse shod, the Spaniards had to make their way through a defile well over a hundred miles long, rising at its summit to some 4,000 meters, covered by a surface of sharp pebbles, and supporting no animal or vegetable life. The height caused mountain sickness, and the cold at night penetrated to the very marrow of the sufferers' bones. Many lost toes and fingers from frostbite, and Mariño de Lobera cites the case of Jeronimo de Castilla, still alive when Lobera was writing, who actually took off his toes with his boots at night and failed to discover their loss until the following morning.

If things were bad for the Spaniards, they were far worse for their Indian followers. Without shoes, practically unclothed, they appear to have died off like flies. Juan de Herrada, who followed the same route a few months later in mid-winter, used the frozen corpses of these wretched natives to build parapets to shelter his own men from the wind. It is commonly stated in contemporary accounts that as many as fifteen thousand Indians entered this pass and that ten thousand failed to emerge from it. There is no means of checking such figures, which do, however, probably afford us at least an approximate idea of the size as well as of the grimness of the undertaking.

When the combined effects of cold, hunger, and bodily suffering were threatening to engulf the whole enterprise in disaster, Almagro decided to go forward himself for help. Selecting a party of twenty, he mounted them on the best available horses, and in three days (two of them spent without food) reached Copiapó. The natives here proved friendly, or at all events cautious, and Almagro had no difficulty in getting together supplies for the relief of his still advancing main force. It emerged from the pass a few days later, with the loss of 170 horses and a number of natives which may have been anything from two to ten thousand. There is no mention of any Spaniard losing his life in this crossing, though eight had already been killed in the earlier fighting.

During the stay in Copiapó, Almagro was able to consolidate his relations with the natives there by making shrewd use of a political feud which had arisen among them. A young chieftain had recently been deposed by one of his clansmen, and Almagro's first act was to restore the youth to his rightful position. With the help of so powerful an ally, it was a simple matter to secure everything required for the refreshment and recuperation of his forces. At the end of a month, all was again in readiness for the continuance of the journey.

Meanwhile Almagro had been making inquiries into the whereabouts of the three Spaniards who had gone forward alone from Tupiza. Mariño de Lobera states that from a Copiapó chieftain he extracted by torture, under which the Indian died, the story that these men had been killed by the natives living further south in the valleys of Huasco and Coquimbo, though certain members of the Copiapó tribe were also implicated. Leaving forty soldiers in Copiapó, Almagro resumed the march south and after passing through Huasco, where he also left a small force, finally arrived in Coquimbo.

Here, after being entertained by the inhabitants for several days, which he used in making secret investigations, Almagro called them to a public meeting. When they were all gathered together, the Spaniards suddenly seized a number of the principal chieftains and kept them under custody until the arrival of the two companies which had been left in Copiapó and Huasco. These brought down with them representative captives from the two places, and to the combined assembly Almagro then addressed himself, explaining in the usual manner the motives of his journey and underlining its religious aspect. He then suddenly asked his listeners why, when he came with such intentions and with no thought to harm them, they had so cruelly murdered his three countrymen. At first the captives merely looked at each other in bewilderment, until it dawned upon them that a matter which they had believed already forgotten was responsible for their captivity. One by one confessions began to be made, and it was not long before the whole story was out. With no further ado, Almagro had thirty of the chieftains publicly burnt at the stake.

While contemporary accounts of this incident vary quite considerably, they are unanimous in regard to the central facts that the three Spaniards were killed and that ten times their number of Indian chieftains were publicly burnt in retaliation. This savage act of reprisal was justified by some of the early chroniclers on the grounds that Almagro had no further trouble with the natives of the three valleys concerned. It is satisfactory to find, however, that the Spanish character of those times was redeemed by others who denounced the atrocious punishment in terms of scandalized horror.

While in Coquimbo, Almagro received the welcome news of the arrival of one of the three ships which Ruy Diaz had been instructed to fit out. The other two, making small headway against the contrary winds and the Humboldt current, had been forced to put in at Chincha and Arica respectively and had become too unseaworthy to continue the voyage. The *San Pedro*, however, reached a point somewhere south of Coquimbo, possibly Los Vilos, and there discharged her badly needed cargo of horsehoes, clothing, and general stores. "The news of the arrival of this vessel," says Oviedo, "caused general rejoicing in the army, because they had no real confidence in ships and sea traffic."

It was at this time that Almagro received news of a Spaniard called Gonzalo Calvo de Barrientos, who was living with the Indians of the Aconcagua valley. This man had had his ears cut off in Peru for some unspecified offense by order of Francisco Pizarro and, being unable to endure the idea of living down so hideous a disfigurement among his own people, had made his way alone to central Chile. There is no account anywhere of how he achieved this astonishing feat, but the unanimity of contemporary writings leaves no doubt either of his existence or of the fact that he had made for himself a position of considerable influence among the *Picunches* of Aconcagua. Largely owing to this man's good offices, Almagro's force made an uneventful march from Coquimbo to the Aconcagua valley, with gifts of grain and meat. A useful date is provided here by Oviedo, who mentions that they "spent Easter" on the way at a point four days' journey from a village "called Lua."[3]

The happy beginning to the relations between the Spaniards and the natives of Aconcagua was destined to be of short duration. As a means of communication with them, Almagro was using Felipillo, his treacherous Peruvian interpreter, who to further an intrigue with one of the royal concubines had contributed in no small measure to Pizarro's decision to execute the Inca Atahualpa. There is no reasonable doubt that Felipillo was in the secret of the rising in Peru and had good cause to view with disfavor the assistance which the Spaniards were receiving from the natives of Aconcagua. He accordingly gave them his own version of everything which it was his duty to translate for Almagro, and succeeded in convincing the chieftains that the Spaniards' real intentions were to assassinate them. He urged them to attack the invaders while they were asleep and could make no use of their horses. His listeners, while not daring to follow such bold advice, nevertheless withdrew from where the Spaniards were situated and hid from the fate which they now understood to be designed for them.

Almagro was upset and at first also greatly puzzled by the sudden desertion. His suspicions, however, were aroused when it was reported that his interpreter had also disappeared. Search parties were at once sent in pursuit, and Felipillo was finally caught in the foothills while making ready his provisions for the journey back to Peru. After a full confession, no doubt extorted from him by the most painful means, he was quartered and the several portions of his body strewn in the public ways.

Even with this example of the invaders' methods so patently exhibited to their mistrustful gaze, the Indian chieftains could still be induced to renew, though with understandably less confidence, their relations with the Spaniards, who now questioned them regarding the nature of the territory lying farther south. The answers were discouraging. The country was said to be populated by the poorest type of natives, living in mean villages of from ten to fifteen huts, and there was no gold. Farther south still, there lived fierce warrior tribes who had once defeated the Incas.

The lack of rich metals and large buildings in the country which the Spaniards saw around them lent every semblance of truth to what they heard from the natives. They were already more than half convinced that the visions which had been conjured up in their minds by the gold presented to them by Villac Umu had no basis in fact, and that their prospects of finding a second Peru were now indeed of the slenderest description.

Nevertheless, after completing the major part of so hazardous a journey, it would have been foolish not to confirm by the relatively small effort of further exploration, the information given by the natives. Almagro accordingly sent out parties in several directions, among them one which discovered what was to become the present port of Valparaiso. The principal of these parties, however, was a force of one hundred Spaniards whom Almagro sent southward under the command of Gomez de Alvarado. He himself remained in Aconcagua to survey his more immediate surroundings and to await the arrival of Ruy Diaz, who had just sent word that he had reached Copiapó after disembarking from the vessel which had been forced into Chincha. Diaz had with him a force of 110 men, which included Almagro's seventeen-year-old son, Don Diego de Almagro the younger, and he had made his way down by the western route through the deserts of Tarapacá, Antofagasta, and Atacama, overcoming not only the natural difficulties of the country but the constant attacks of the natives who were now all in open revolt. He joined Almagro not long after Alvarado's departure.

Gomez de Alvarado left Aconcagua in July and advanced doggedly southward in the depths of what seems to have been an exceptionally severe winter. He met no opposition until he reached the river Maule, where a group of Indians tried to dispute his passage but were easily repulsed by a few troops under Martin Monje. Continuing southward, he had no further difficulty until reaching the junction of the rivers Nuble and Itata, where Spaniard and Araucanian gazed upon each other for the first time.

The total number of those who fought that day was as nothing to the thousands of lives which were to be sacrificed in the territory for the next three centuries. Reinoguelen, an obscure Indian skirmish too small for notice in any self-respecting history of warfare, has a drama which is lacking in many a more spectacular clash of arms.

Supremely unaware of the significance of the moment, the Spaniards made ready in their customary businesslike manner for the coming struggle. When it came, they were undoubtedly startled by its quality. The Araucanians, while lacking the organization they were to display later, and laboring under the incalculable handicap of never having previously seen horses, sustained the vigor of their massed attacks for several hours before being forced to withdraw. They lost many dead and left a hundred prisoners behind them. Nevertheless they succeeded in killing two Spaniards, a figure which may seem small but, on current native performance, was extremely good going for a first introduction to cavalry.

No more eloquent comment upon the fight is needed than Gomez de Alvarado's immediate decision to retrace his steps northward. Though the poorness of the country and the foulness of the weather certainly offered him little inducement to proceed further, he cannot have failed to be influenced by the unusual fighting qualities of the people he now found in front of him. After an uneventful march, he reached Aconcagua in September. "Since the land was not teeming with gold, he found no good in it" is the simple comment of Cristobal de Molina.

Alvarado's report stripped away whatever illusions may still have been left to the Spaniards regarding Chile's resources. During his absence, the territory adjacent to Aconcagua had been explored in several directions, and certain of the Indian gold mines had been discovered, "as well worked as if Spaniards had been engaged in them, and so worked out that the best pan produced a bare twelve grains" (Oviedo). This was the reality of the adventurers' dreams of finding another Peru full of cities, roads, rich farms, and fabulous mines. The gamble had failed, and whatever Almagro himself may have wanted, his followers' desires were clear and manifest. There was only one Peru in the world, and they had become extremely anxious to return and obtain their share of it. They reminded their leader of the vast amount of money which he had invested in the enterprise and pointed out the impossibility of obtaining its return from the kind of country they were in. "If you were to die here," they said, "you would have nothing to leave to your son but the name of Don Diego."[4]

The decision to return once taken, Almagro had no thought but to be back in Peru as soon as possible, a determination which had disastrous consequences for the Chilean natives who were pressed into service for the return journey. Cristobal de Molina, who is extremely severe on his countrymen for their treatment of the Indians, treatment which he witnessed and is constantly telling us that he devoutly wishes he had been spared, says that Almagro now allowed his followers complete license. "No Spaniard left Chile," he goes on, "who did not bring Indians in bonds; he who had chains, in chains, while others made stout halters from hides and took numbers of stocks along to imprison them at night; and it was their custom on this march to keep the wretched Indians under observation to prevent their fleeing, and for this purpose they always herded them on to an open piece of ground, and if any Indian moved it was inferred that he was trying to get away, and those who were on watch beat him with sticks . . . There was one Spaniard on this journey who put twelve Indians into a chain and flattered himself that they all died in it; when one Indian had expired, to frighten the rest and to avoid taking the chain off them, he cut off his head so as to release him without opening the padlock which he controlled with a key; it was quite the usual custom, if some miserable Indian grew tired or sick, not to free him from the chain until he actually died because, it was said, if they let one go all the rest would grow sick or tired so as to be let go also, and they found this a quite singular argument." One can merely add that the logic is flawless.

Widely distinct as are the points of view of contemporary writers on the subject, some condemning and others pleading the necessity of the Spanish ruthlessness, they are all in

substantial agreement regarding the fact of the brutal treatment to which the natives were subjected. From the moral
standpoint of today, no justification whatever can be attempted. In considering the matter, however, it has to be borne in
mind that the Indian's tremendous inferiority made deceit and
treachery the only effective weapons which he could use to
defend himself, weapons which would very soon seem to justify
the sternest repressive measures in the minds of his conquerors.
Moreover, if the Spaniards were infinitely more powerful individually, they were pitifully weak in numbers and could afford
to take no chances on the side of leniency. In addition they had
absolute need of the services of the Indians, without whose
assistance their amazing marches could never have been undertaken. In the journey back to Peru, their very lives depended
on the backbreaking transportation demanded of the natives
who would certainly not carry out such a task of their own free
will. The origin of this vicious circle is to be found not in any
exceptional brutality on the part of the Spaniards, but in the
fact that the New World had to be discovered and explored. If
this last postulate is accepted, it is difficult to avoid the acceptance with it of much that the exploration necessarily entailed. Without attempting to justify the Spaniards' cruelty on
moral grounds, it must still be said in fairness that they probably behaved no better and no worse than other civilized men
have behaved in similar circumstances in other parts of the
world.

Ahead of the main body, Almagro set out with thirty
horsemen for Copiapó. Here he found Orgoñez, who had
brought down seventy-five men, and Herrada with a company
of eighty-eight. Both had followed the same route as Almagro
himself and had suffered in a similar manner. Herrada had

raised his force in Lima with the intention of coming down by sea. Hearing, however, that Hernando Pizarro had returned from Spain, and knowing that he was the bearer of Almagro's letters of appointment, he decided to return to Cuzco and carry these documents down to the new governor himself. Though continually put off by Pizarro on one pretext after another, he finally obtained possession of the papers and set out by the eastern route. In the terrible passage over the Andes, it was he who had the bodies of the natives who had already died there piled into parapets to shield his own men from the cold, while the frozen horses of the preceding parties supplied him with meat. The Spaniards of this company actually reached the pitch of drawing their knives on each other in disputing which were to enjoy such delicacies as the brains and tongues of the long dead beasts.

After handing Almagro his dispatches, Herrada soon brought his leader up to date on events in Peru. He told him of the extension of Pizarro's province seventy leagues southwards, and of his consequent claim that Cuzco lay indisputably within his borders. The attempt to withhold his rival's letters of appointment from Herrada was easily attributed to a desire to keep Almagro in Chile for as long as possible and to make every preparation to ensure that he should never obtain possession of the Inca capital. Finally, there was the news that all Peru was in revolt and that the Inca Manco had laid siege to the town which was the principal bone of contention between the opposing Spanish factions. If there had been any last doubts in Almagro's mind about the desirability of re-turning to Peru, all this news immediately removed them.

A choice had again to be made between the alternative routes, of both of which the different members of the expedition had now had practical experience. The Spaniards decided to pray for guidance on this point during mass, and on leaving the building which had served them for a Church, found that they were unanimous in selecting the desert.

The local knowledge which had been obtained by Ruy Diaz's company was turned to good account. Almagro had guanaco-hide wineskins and every other available container filled with water, and after gathering together the necessary provisions, sent forward a digging party to open up the water holes which existed at a number of points along the route, thus increasing the flow of water. Once he had received reassuring messages from the advance party, he began to send forward his men five and six at a time. Each water hole was sufficient to supply just that number of Spaniards, together with their horses and native retinue. It was necessary carefully to space out the times of departure, since one party had always to have vacated a water hole before the succeeding one reached it.

The principal difficulty of adopting this plan lay in the danger of annihilation by native attacks to which such small groups were necessarily exposed. To guard against it, Almagro sent eighty men by sea in the vessel which had reached Coquimbo, with instructions to await the arrival of the small parties in San Pedro de Atacama and so enable them to emerge from the desert under the powerful protection. The plan succeeded admirably, and the whole force made their way safely through to the assigned meeting place.

After a short rest, the march was continued through the Antofagasta and Tarapacá deserts, and Arequipa was reached early in 1537. The only loss recorded came to Gonzalo Fernandez de Oviedo y Valdés, one of the principal sources of our information, whose son was drowned during the crossing of an unnamed river.

Almagro's first act on reaching Arequipa was to try to make contact with the rebellious Inca Manco, who still had a large force under arms near Cuzco. The two men had been on friendly terms in the past, and Almagro hoped to be able to deal with the present dangerous state of affairs by peaceful negotiation. His emissaries met with a good reception at the hands of the Inca, who complained that his main reason for revolt was the behavior of Pizarro, who "had treated him as a dog" and continually called on him to produce more gold under threat of burning at the stake. He agreed to meet Almagro in person in the vale of Yucay, whither the Spaniard accordingly advanced with half his force, stationing the remainder at Urcos, some six leagues from Cuzco.

Hernando Pizarro, who was now in command in Cuzco, marched out from the city with a small force in the direction of Urcos to discover what this sudden appearance of Almagro's company portended. When he learned that they meant to claim Cuzco, he quickly withdrew inside its gates and made preparations to resist.

The meeting between soldiers of the two Spanish parties near Urcos had not gone unnoticed by the Indians, who reported the occurrence to Manco. The Inca at once suspected that the invaders were in agreement and that the meeting at Yucay was no more than an attempt to take him between two fires. He determined, therefore, to spring the surprise himself, and fell upon Almagro with an army amounting to fifteen thousand warriors. If he hoped to take the veteran fighters from Chile unawares, he suffered a sharp disappointment. Rallying briskly to the challenge, the Spaniards routed the Peruvians with tremendous slaughter, inflicting upon them a blow from which they, in fact, never recovered.

Almagro now served his demands upon the Municipality of Cuzco for the city to be delivered to him, alleging that it formed part of his province. The Municipality gave the noncommittal reply that before agreeing to these demands, they would have to consult certain pilots who had a more precise knowledge than themselves of the exact geographical position of Cuzco. At the same time a truce was arranged between the contending armies, each agreeing to remain quietly where it was.

Almagro's men soon suspected that Hernando Pizarro was breaking this truce by using it to perfect his defensive preparations. They were no doubt encouraged in their entertainment of such suspicions by the cold, wet weather to which they were exposed while Pizarro's men lived snugly inside the city. So great became their insistence upon their leader's taking what they declared to be no more than his own that he finally allowed himself to be persuaded to put an end to the truce. On the night of April 8, 1537, he suddenly attacked the city and quickly had it under control. Hernando and Gonzalo Pizarro became Almagro's prisoners. Not long afterwards, on July 12 of the same year, Almagro scored a brilliant victory over Francisco Pizarro's lieutenant, Alonso de Alvarado, on the banks of the river Abancay, capturing an entire force of five hundred men, just about equal in size to his own army. This victory, however, was to be the high-water mark of his success.

A series of negotiations was thereafter conducted between Pizarro and Almagro and ended with the final verdict pronounced by Fray Francisco de Bovadilla, to whom both parties had agreed to submit their dispute for arbitration. By its principal terms, Cuzco was to remain in Almagro's hands until the exact boundary line between the two provinces could be determined, while Hernando Pizarro was to be released on the formal understanding that he would leave the country within six weeks. Gonzalo Pizarro had already contrived to escape from Almagro's clutches and so did not come within the scope of the agreement. When Orgoñez, Almagro's loyal lieutenant, heard the terms of the award, he exclaimed, lifting up his beard and passing his finger across his throat, "Orgoñez, Orgoñez, your friendship with Almagro will cost you your head."[5] He had taken exactly the measure of the Pizarros.

No sooner was the award known, and Hernando Pizarro released, than Francisco began openly to make his preparations for the final elimination of Almagro. He entrusted the leadership of his army not merely to Gonzalo, but to Hernando as well, absolving his elder brother from his solemn promise to leave the country, since the undertaking had been given "contrary to the interests of the Crown."[6] The Pizarros had their own ways of reconciling their actions with their consciences. Finally, Francisco denounced the existence of all agreements with Almagro, and notified his now thoroughly awakened opponent that he must vacate Cuzco and the province of New Castile or be held responsible for the consequences.

There was nothing for it but either to leave Peru or to fight it out. Almagro's first thought was to ensure the possession of Cuzco. In the race to secure the Guaitara passes, Pizarro was too quick for his rival, whose prompt occupation of this approach to the city might have delayed the issue indefinitely. Battle in the neighborhood of Cuzco itself was all that remained. Orgoñez was now in full command, Almagro being prostrate with the effects of what is believed to have been syphilis. He was actually forced to halt for three whole weeks in Bilcas on his way back to the Inca capital, so severe had become the effects of his complaint.

Orgoñez chose Las Salinas, some three or four miles outside Cuzco, as the scene of the final struggle. He has been criticized for choosing marshy ground where his main strength, his cavalry, would be hampered. He had, however, a force of not more than five hundred men to oppose to the seven hundred supporters of Pizarro, and being on the defensive, he had a natural inclination to choose ground which would embarrass the greater offensive power of his opponents.

On April 26, 1538, the battle of Las Salinas took place before a large audience. The natives, realizing that their oppressors were coming to blows, had turned up in force to witness an event which could be of no benefit to any but themselves. Almagro watched his last battle from a litter, in which he was carried to a point of vantage. Inevitably the superior forces of the Pizarros made their weight felt, and in less than two hours Almagro had the bitterness of seeing his men in full flight for Cuzco. Here he himself was captured shortly afterward and confined in irons in the very apartment where he had held Hernando Pizarro a prisoner.

Hernando had heard before the battle that Almagro was desperately ill and is quoted as having exclaimed, "God cannot do me so great a wrong as to let him die before he falls into my hands." His attitude toward Almagro immediately after the battle fully bears out this spirit of vindictiveness. While secretly and most actively preparing a case against him, he appears to have deliberately lulled him into a sense of false security in order the more fully to relish the horror which would be felt by a confident and convalescent captive at the sudden knowledge of inevitable doom. He paid Almagro a visit and told him that he was merely awaiting arrival of Francisco in order to release him, promising to accept the responsibility for taking this step himself if there were any protracted delay in his brother's arrival. He even kept his prisoner supplied with good food from his own table, and in short did everything possible to restore Almagro both mentally and physically to a state where sentence and execution would be felt as exquisitely as possible.

Meanwhile two whole months had been spent in completing the case against the unsuspecting captive, and it finally comprised no less than 4,000 pages. Anybody who had a claim against the unfortunate man was most cordially invited to prefer it, though the principal charges on which he was convicted, in his absence and without his knowledge or any chance to defend himself, were those of making war on his sovereign and so causing many Spanish deaths, of conspiring with the Inca, and finally of forcibly seizing Cuzco from the hands of a properly appointed royal governor. The sentence passed was death as a traitor; he was to be executed by public beheading in the great square of Cuzco.

Almagro was stunned when the sentence was communicated to him by a priest. When he was able fully to comprehend the hideousness of the end which now stared him in the face, he asked for an interview with Hernando Pizarro, an interview entirely to his captor's taste. "Do not kill me, for the love of God," Almagro begged. "Remember that I have never shed the blood of your friends or relations, even though I have had them in my power and entirely at my mercy; recollect that I have been the principal support on which Francisco Pizarro, your beloved brother, has raised himself to that summit of honor and wealth at which he now finds himself; look at how old, thin, and gouty I am; allow me to live, even though it be in prison, for the few sad days that remain to me for the repentance of my sins."

"I should be pleased," replied Pizarro, "for your old age to be spared such an end, provided this kingdom could remain at peace while you live. You are not the only man in this world who has died, nor will others be lacking to die the death reserved for you. In a word, make no doubt that the last day of your existence has arrived; and since God has done you the mercy of making you a Christian, commend your soul to Him and ask forgiveness for your sins . . . You are a soldier and bear an illustrious name; this is no time for an exhibition of weakness; I am amazed that a man of your spirit should have so great a fear of death . . . Confess yourself, for nothing can now save you."[7]

The words of his cold-blooded captor removed whatever last hopes Almagro may still have clung to. Once convinced that his doom was inevitable, he devoted himself calmly to his last preparations. Appointing his son, Don Diego the younger, to succeed him in his office, he made Charles V his residuary legatee, while assuring his sovereign that a great deal was still due to him in his account with Pizarro. He shrewdly hoped by this one stroke both to engage King Charles' sympathy on behalf of his heir, and at the same time to ensure that the monarch would now have the strongest personal motives for instituting a thorough audit of Pizarro's books. One of the witnesses who signed this codicil was a certain Pedro de Valdivia, Pizarro's quartermaster at the battle of Las Salinas.

On the same day, Almagro was strangled in his cell. His

body was then taken to the public square and beheaded in accordance with the sentence. His principal mourners were Hernando and Gonzalo Pizarro, rigorously dressed in black. It is some consolation to know that when Hernando Pizarro finally returned to Spain, Almagro's loyal friends were able to have him thrown into prison, where he remained for twenty years. When he finally emerged, he found himself "alone in the world, without friends or enemies, for both the one and the other had departed from earth before him."[8]

By his own directions, Almagro's body was buried in the chapel of the Convent of Our Lady of Mercy in Cuzco. It was to be only a few years before his son, the only child upon whom he had lavished all the affection of which his warm-hearted nature was capable, was laid to rest in the same grave. Caught up in the toils of his father's feud, this ill-starred youth met an exactly similar end before he had attained to full manhood. Prior to his execution, he made the request that his father's body be disinterred in order that his own might be buried beneath. There is that in the simple request which must heighten our estimation of both men.

3

Pedro de Valdivia
Prepares to
Set Out
for Chile

There now steps upon the scene of Chilean conquest the remarkable figure who was to beget a new nation. By an odd twist of fate, it was from among the principal instruments of the final ruin and destruction of Chile's first explorer, Don Diego de Almagro, that her real conqueror emerged. The contrast between these two characters is as great as that between the results of their two expeditions. Almagro's heart, full of the golden glamor of Peru, as never really in the job. His successor, once he had decided to go south, subordinated his every action to the purpose of founding the new country. His constancy in the face of every difficulty which could be produced by the combined effects of lack of funds and following, bitter fighting, famine, homesickness, treachery, and sedition was such as at times calls for not merely our admiration but our utter amazement and awe. When he eventually succumbed to his Indian foes, whose military greatness he probably never fully realized, his wife was already on her way to join him. The fact of his having sent for her is the clearest indication of his satisfaction with a sound beginning. Perhaps he knew when he died that the foundations of his monument, the "Fame and Memory of me" which it was his proudest desire to leave behind him, had been deeply and solidly laid.

Pedro de Valdivia was born round about the year 1502 in the district of La Serena in Spain. Fourteen villages have competed for the honor of being his birthplace, without any conclusive result. Historical evidence has been produced in support of most of them, but principally on behalf of Castuera, Zalamea, Villanueva, and Campanario. Little is known with any certainty regarding his parentage, the only definite statement on the subject being that of Mariño de Lobera, who describes him as "the legitimate son of Pedro Oncas de Melo, a Portuguese, hidalgo, and Isabel Gutierrez de Valdivia[1] of the village of Campanario in Extremadura, of very noble descent."[2] What appears certain is that he was of good family and had received an education well above the average of his day.

From the age of nineteen onward, he followed a military career and, to use the words which he himself wrote to his representatives at the Spanish Court, had followed tradition "like a good soldier and in imitiation of my forbears who were and still are employed in this same career of arms . . . I served His Majesty in Italy in the time of Prospero Colona and the Marquess of Pescara until the time of the latter's death, which occurred at the taking of the state of Milan . . . and I served in Flanders when His Majesty was in Valenciana and the King of France came against it."

He left the service in 1525 and married Marina Ortiz de Gaete in the village of Zalamea. There is no record of the next ten years of his life, which we must suppose him to have led in a quiet domestic manner in his village home.

"I came," he says in the letter already referred to, "to the

Indies in 1535, and I spent one year in assisting in the discovery and conquest of Venezuela." Leaving his wife and family, whom he was destined never to see again, he made the voyage in the company of a lifelong friend and supporter, Jeronimo de Alderete, later to be one of his principal followers in the expedition to Chile. The Venezuelan adventure, however, held out small hope of glory or advancement to a man of Valdiva's ambition, and he welcomed the opportunity of enrollment in Diego de Fuenmayor's force of four hundred men sent by the Royal Audience of Santo Domingo to Peru in response to the call from Francisco Pizarro. Here his high military qualities were quickly recognized, with the result, as we have seen, that he became Quartermaster General in Pizarro's army.

For his services at the battle of Las Salinas and in the subsequent pacification of the colony, he was rewarded by Pizarro with the immensely valuable estate of "La Canela," and a silver mine in Porco. The former of these two properties alone was estimated to produce an income equivalent to £120,000 per year,[3] and was later sufficient to reward the services of three separate people. At the age of thirty-seven Valdivia had achieved a position of such wealth and prestige as was equaled only by that of Pizarro himself. In making any assessment of Valdivia's character, it is important to bear in mind the enormous amount of material riches which he renounced in order to undertake his expedition southward.

At this time Pizarro was being besieged with requests for commissions to lead exploratory expeditions in all directions except to Chile. The reputation of this country, once rumored to be a land of so much wealth and promise, had suffered severely from Almagro's abortive attempt to bring it under

Spanish control. Where the fabulously wealthy *Adelantado*, with his magnificently equipped force of five hundred men, had failed, there were small prospects indeed of success for the lesser captains of the day with their relatively insignificant resources. To Pizarro's astonishment, Valdivia applied for precisely this commission.

Valdivia confesses in his correspondence that his friends expressed doubts of his sanity when they learned of his intentions. They could scarcely credit the folly of his surrendering the security of his vast estates, and an income almost as large as Pizarro's own,[4] for the purpose of committing himself to an undertaking which all believed doomed to failure. They had failed to observe that Valdivia was not just a vulgar adventurer, such as were not a few of themselves, and that the mere accumulation of worldly possessions could in itself afford him no more than a passing satisfaction. After obtaining everything which the vast majority of the Spaniards had left their country to seek, he deliberately cast it aside as of no account, in order to face the dangers and hardships of an expedition which even in the unlikely event of success seemed to offer no hope of any considerable material reward. Chile now lacked even the glamor of the unknown. She had been stripped of all the exciting possibilities which had attracted a man with the temperament of Almagro. It was with a good knowledge both of her lack of mineral wealth and of the excellent fighting qualities of her inhabitants that Valdivia chose her. His purpose was to found and build, not to despoil. Chile lay, in the picturesque phrasing of Francisco Encina, a virgin country, awaiting only the embrace of civilized man to become abundantly fertile. Pedro de Valdivia was that civilized man, and therein lies his real title to fame.

Pizarro granted him the commission in April 1539, and he immediately set about making his preparations. His first difficulties were financial ones. Unlimited credit could have been secured by the possessor of the "La Canela" estate, but the doors were shut to the leader of an expedition to Chile.[5] Francisco Pizarro had granted Valdivia his commission, but he gave him no financial aid either from his own private funds or from the public treasury.[6] Valdivia could raise only some 15,000 *Castellanos* on his own account, and it seemed that his expedition was doomed for lack of money before it had even begun to be organized. After six months of fruitless effort, when perhaps even Valdivia himself may have begun to lose heart, his perseverance was rewarded and the position saved by a merchant newly arrived from Spain, Francisco Martinez, who offered a number of horses, arms, and other equipment to the value of some 9,000 *Castellanos,* on the condition that a partnership be formed and that he receive half the profits of the enterprise. It is worth noticing that Francisco Martinez put his own value on the goods which he contributed, and that when the partnership was dissolved some years afterward, the referees reduced Valdivia's indebtedness to 5,000 *Castellanos.* The importance of the loan at this stage, however, was not its intrinsic value, but the fact that it came from Martinez. The backing of this wealthy merchant soon enabled Valdivia to obtain further credit, amounting in all to some 70,000 *Castellanos.*

The monetary problem being temporarily settled, the next difficulty had to be overcome. Valdivia appeared to be the only man in Peru with any desire to go to Chile. His hopes of obtaining a sufficient following were centered mainly upon the discredited partisans of Almagro, who could expect little future in Peru and of whom Pizarro had an obvious interest in ridding himself. Unfortunately, those who had least desire to see Chile were those who had been there before.[7]

It so happened, however, that two of Pizarro's captains, Pedro de Candia and Diego de Rojas, had received commissions from him to lead expeditions into the territories known as "Los Chunchos" and "Los Chiriguanos," which today form part of Bolivia. Both men had recruited their following mainly from among the Almagro faction. The two expeditions proved equally disastrous, and it was to the returning survivors from them that Valdivia must be presumed to have got messages through, since it was they who, as we shall see, were to link up with him on the way south, and eventually formed some two-thirds of his total strength of 150 men.

These formidable of lack of funds and followers having been fairly overcome, the third and only possible remaining difficulty of importance presented itself. His own right to the leadership of the expedition was challenged from an entirely unexpected quarter.

Sancho de Hoz, destined to play the villain of the piece in the completest possible fashion, had recently returned from Spain after an absence of four years. He had received 4,400 *Castellanos* as his share of the Inca Atahualpa's ransom, at the distribution of which he is mentioned as being the notary's assistant. He was subsequently appointed to be Pizarro's private secretary, and it was in this capacity that he obtained leave of absence in April, 1535, and made the voyage home. There he married an aristocratic wife, Doña Giomar de Aragon, who appears to have had considerable influence at court. After squandering his share of the ransom, Sancho decided to return to the new continent to repair his fortunes, and had by this time sufficiently gained his sovereign's ear to obtain from him a commission to explore and to govern all islands off the west coast not yet under Spanish control and all the territory lying to the south of the Magellan Straits.[8] He had now reappeared on the scene, therefore, as Governor for the King, titularly on a footing with Pizarro himself and taking precedence over Pedro de Valdivia, who was merely a Governor's lieutenant. He claimed the right as King's Governor to take charge of the expedition to Chile.

Valdivia was in no position to insist on his greater claims. He was entirely dependent upon Pizarro, who had appointed him and could revoke his nomination at pleasure. Furthermore, the execution of Almagro had greatly weakened Pizarro's position at the Spanish Court, and he was at this time particularly anxious not to do anything which might be construed as running counter to his sovereign's express desires. He accordingly suggested a compromise by which Sancho de Hoz should become a partner of Valdivia and Martinez, on the condition that within the space of four months Sancho should provide fifty horses, two hundred breastplates, and two complete shiploads of other equipment required for the expedition. An act of agreement on these lines was finally signed in Prizarro's dining room.[9]

The loss of this document, or its deliberate destruction by Pedro de Valdivia as is more generally believed, has led to a good deal of controversy as to whether Valdivia or Sancho was in fact appointed the supreme leader of the enterprise. Certain of its clauses only have been preserved in the act of annulment which Sancho de Hoz was later to be induced to sign in San Pedro de Atacama, and these are clauses not unfavorable to Valdivia's claims. The act of annulment, however, was drawn up at Valdivia's instigation by his own partisans, and was presumably designed to put his own position in the most favorable light. These circumstances have led to the assertion by certain eminent authorities that Sancho de Hoz, not Pedro de Valdivia, was the legitimate leader of the expedition, contingently upon his fulfilling his undertaking to supply the stipulated amount of equipment within a period of four months.

The subject is of insufficient importance, so far as its practical effects on subsequent history are concerned, to be pursued in any detail here. We submit the opinion, however, that Crescente Errazuriz, in an exhaustive study of the problem, has in fact decided the issue in favor of Valdivia on two points alone.

Firstly, La Gasca, reporting on Pedro de Valdivia's trial in Peru, and having himself sifted all the available evidence, writes, "Pero Sancho had no commission whatsoever which might support his pretensions to the conquest of Chile."[10] He adds that it was principally with the object of settling his doubts on this point that he recalled Valdivia to Peru for examination.

Secondly, and perhaps more importantly, Sancho de Hoz nowhere makes any definite claim to the leadership of the expedition on the strength of the lost document. He continually refers in a vague way to his Royal Commission, which, however, precisely excludes the whole of Chile by reference to the various Governorships which then legally comprised it, and entitles him only to explore and govern such islands off the coast as had hitherto remained undiscovered, and the territory lying to the south of the Magellan Straits. It is incredible that

52

he should have refrained from mentioning, let alone showing, to Valdivia's followers a document which only after its disa-appearance has given rise to the claim that he was the contingently appointed leader and head of the expedition.

Valdivia, finding his third difficulty disposed of by the agreement of Sancho de Hoz to remain behind and gather together the necessary supplies, was now free to set forth. In doing so, he provided himself with the opportunity for making what must surely rank as one of the greatest understatements on record.

4

The
March
Southward

"In January, 1540," says Valdivia, "I left Cuzco, not in such force as was adequate."[1] Bernal de Martin states concisely, eighteen years later, that when Valdivia set out, he was accompanied by exactly seven Spaniards, of whom Martin himself was one.[2] Seventeen others certainly joined him shortly afterward, some probably on the outskirts of the city and others on the road a few days later. The fact remains, however, that considered as a force raised for the conquest of a vast territory such as Chile, the initial company was not by any form of calculation "adequate."

In addition, he had collected about a thousand Indians to serve as porters and camp followers. These Indians were regarded as hardly better than animals, and are usually referred to in the old documents simply as "Pieces of service." In the accounts of the endless battles with the Chilean natives, the casualties of the "Pieces," if mentioned at all, are recorded only after those of the horses, which were scarce and of far greater importance to their Spanish masters.

A woman, also, accompanied the expedition. Inés de Suarez, a widow whose husband's name has not been preserved, had become Pedro de Valdivia's mistress, and preferred sharing with him the dangers and sufferings of his great undertaking to being left behind in Peru without him. This fact would in itself afford ample proof of the sincerity of the relationship so far as she was concerned. There are, however, a hundred witnesses in contemporary records to add their separate testimony to the greatness of her character, and give the lie to those who would lay too much emphasis upon the single fact of an illicit union. When she was finally forced to leave Valdivia, in order that he might fulfill one of the principal conditions of his being confirmed in his governorship, she did so with the greatest dignity and self-effacement. Rodrigo de Quiroga, among the most distinguished of Valdivia's captains, married her, and it was as his wife that she eventually became what it was never in Valdivia's power to make her, the consort of the governor of the colony. No woman ever had as good a claim to the position, or filled it to greater purpose. Following her pioneer's destiny in an obscure outpost of Spanish conquest, Inés de Suarez is not unfit to be ranked among the notable women of her day.

Profiting by Almagro's experience, Valdivia chose the route by which his predecessor had returned. Of the first two or three months of the journey, employed in the march from Cuzco to Tarapacá, by way of Arequipa, Moquegua, and Tacna, few details have been preserved. There are references to lack of food and water, fatigue, and excessive cold, but little in the way of particular incident. The Indians had been given advance tidings of the expedition by the Inca Manco, and had been instructed to adopt what we may call a "scorched earth" policy. They appear to have carried out with far greater thoroughness in this instance a general plan of campaign which had already given excellent results in the case of the previous expedition under Almagro.

The first serious setback was the death, within a few days of setting out, of Valdivia's chief of staff, Alvar Gomez, a blood brother of Diego de Almagro himself. He was replaced by Pero Gomez de Don Benito, a loyal soldier who had the advantage of having accompanied Almagro and so acquired a firsthand knowledge of the route and the territory in general. The loss of Alvar Gomez was followed some time later by the severe wounding of Valdivia's merchant partner, Francisco Martinez, in Tacama, presumably during a skirmish with the natives of the district. Valdivia had no option but to send him back to Arequipa, detaching two soldiers, Juan de Almonacid and Bautista Ventura, to act as an escort. The former had instructions to rejoin the expedition as soon as possible. The latter, a brother of the wounded man, was to stay in Peru and organize the transport of additional supplies by sea.

Of his twenty-four men, Valdivia had now lost the four mentioned above, and he reached Tarapacá with the remaining twenty. Here he decided to await the long hoped for reinforcements, without which it would have been madness to proceed further. An anxious period of delay ensued. Sancho de Hoz had given no sign of life, nor had any of the forces returning from Bolivia so far got through. In desperation Valdivia decided to send Pero Gomez de Don Benito to Collao in search of men and supplies. The mission was a dismal failure, and Gomez was destined to return without a single recruit.

In his absence, however, the whole picture became greatly changed. Rodrigo de Araya arrived with a force of sixteen, bringing the total in camp to thirty-six. Not long afterward, between seventy and eighty more men appeared on the scene, principally persuaded and led thereto by Francisco de Villagra, possibly the most notable figure in the Chilean history of this period after Pedro de Valdivia himself. Villagra had been Chief of Staff in turn to both Pedro de Candia and Diego de Rojas in their disastrous expeditions into Los Chunchos and Los Chiriguanos, to which we have already referred, and it was he who helped and encouraged the survivors to respond to Valdivia's call and join the expedition to Chile.

Among these newcomers were Jeronimo de Alderete, later to be Governor-elect, Pedro de Villagra, who was to act as Governor for two years, Juan Jufré, Juan Fernandez de Alderete, Juan de Cuevas, and other captains of note. Among them also was Rodrigo Gonzales de Marmolejo, later to be Chile's first bishop.

On Pero Gomez's return from his fruitless errand, Valdivia decided to renew the march after an enforced rest of two months. Once again a long tract of desert had to be traversed, with equipment and supplies. For a modern caravan to attempt the task would be a severe test of organization and endurance. The question of exactly how the Spaniards managed to do it beggars the imagination. It must suffice our curiosity that the soldiers and their horses were able to transport themselves, and that the "Pieces" were coerced into carrying everything else.

Shortly before reaching Atacama the Smaller (possibly Chiu-Chiu) at the beginning of June, Valdivia went forward with a small force of ten horsemen to make preparations and gather supplies in Atacama the Greater (probably San Pedro de Atacama). In doing so, he unwittingly saved himself from reasonably certain assassination at the hands of his partner, Sancho de Hoz.

This lamentable figure, after signing his agreement with Valdivia, had gone straightway to Lima to obtain the stipulated supplies. What he got instead was to be thrown into prison for debt. His creditors soon realized, however, that his imprisonment would not help them to their money, and they released him therefore to enable him to collect the necessary funds. In their place, he collected a few close friends and concocted with them a desperate plot to obtain the command of the Chilean expedition.

One of these friends, Gonzalo de los Rios, with a troop of some twenty followers at his disposal, declared later that he separated from the conspirators on the road when he saw the real nature of Sancho's intentions. According to this same witness, Sancho openly declared that he had no hope of fulfilling his part of the agreement with Valdivia, and that his only remedy lay in violence. He was also seen to buy three daggers in Arequipa.

A definite plan was finally agreed upon. Sancho himself, together with Antonio de Ulloa and Juan de Guzman, were to go forward and join the expedition, while Alonso de Chinchilla was to follow more slowly in order to gather fresh recruits on the way. Sancho and his two companions were to enter the camp, and while the former engaged Valdivia in greeting by throwing his arms around his neck, the others would plunge their daggers into their intended victim's helpless body.

After Valdivia's departure, the camp had halted for the night at a point about twelve leagues from Atacama the Smaller. In the small hours, Sancho de Hoz, accompanied by Juan de Guzman, Antonio de Ulloa, and Diego Lopez de

Avalos, approached the tent of a soldier called Bartolomé Diaz, in the apparent belief that it was Valdivia's. Discovering their mistake, they inquired for Valdivia, and Diaz led the party, now reinforced by Juan de Guzman's brother Diego, to the leader's habitation.

Without speaking or using any light, Sancho and his companions entered the tent and felt about for the bed. Inés de Suarez, awakened by the disturbance, cried out, "Who are you? What do you want?"

"Where is the Captain?" asked Sancho in his turn.

"He is not here," replied Inés. "What do you want with him? Who are you? Tell me at once who you are!"

Sancho knew that the opportunity had already passed, and that anything but straightforwardness would now be not merely useless but dangerous. "Madam, it is Pero Sancho de Hoz," he replied.

"And how comes it, Sir, that a man such as yourself is found entering another's tent? The matter has an odd look."

"Since I am the Captain's servant," replied Sancho, "Madam has no need of surprise."[3]

Sancho de Hoz had deceived no one. At Francisco de Villagra's trial, a whole series of witnesses refer to the attempted assassination as an accepted fact, which indeed neither at this time nor later is ever called into question. Inés de Suarez, nevertheless, considered it prudent to dissimulate, and even gave supper to the conspirators, after sending word to Pero Gomez de Don Benito. The latter, on receiving the message, was in two minds regarding his proper course of action. On the one hand, he was as convinced as any of Sancho's real intentions and had good reason to fear that delay in taking strong disciplinary action might be fatal. Sancho would undoubtedly use any interval for canvassing support for his pretensions among the more disaffected members of the expedition, who in their turn would be encouraged by anything which could be construed as weakness on the part of the temporary leader. Worse still, the boldness of Sancho's attempt made it plain that he had good reasons for believing that these disaffected members were something more than a small minority, and that he in fact already felt confident of obtaining substantial support. Against these considerations had to be placed the obvious danger of taking drastic action against a man with as much influence at the Spanish court as was possessed by Sancho de Hoz. Pero Gomez not unwisely decided to temporize, and contented himself with sending two soldiers posthaste to recall Valdivia to the scene of action.

The march was resumed next day. As Gomez de Don Benito had feared, Sancho and his friends took advantage of Valdivia's absence to sow the seeds of discord. One of Sancho's partisans, a scheming intriguer by the name of Antonio de Pastrana, circulated the dangerous rumor that Sancho had come to distribute the rewards of land and Indian labor among the expedition's members, in accordance with the supposed terms of his commission from Pizarro. Pastrana was sufficiently careful, however, to see that the ostensible source of the rumor was not himself, but Antonio de Ulloa, already implicated in the plot of assassination. After a whole day of this kind of performance, Sancho's insolence had by evening reached a pitch where he felt capable of reprimanding Gomez de Don Benito for his arrangements in the disposal of the camp. Addressing him by his official title, he exclaimed, "This camp is badly laid out. See that it is not so arranged another night."

Gomez de Don Benito, if we may believe his own version,[4]

was in no mood to tolerate this piece of impertinence, and retorted, "Do not repeat that observation, because I recognize no debt of obedience to you, but only to Don Pedro de Valdivia, and if you do repeat it, I shall hang you from the nearest tree."

In the midst of this highly explosive situation, Valdivia himself arrived the following morning, accompanied by Francisco de Aguirre, who had been awaiting him in Atacama the Greater for the past two months. Aguirre had himself taken part in the expedition to Los Chunchos and with a force of fifteen horsemen and ten infantry had fought his way out without the loss of a single man. In addition to Aguirre himself this welcome reinforcement included Rodrigo de Quiroga, whom we have already noted as future Governor of the colony and husband-to-be of Inés de Suarez.

As though nothing whatever had happened, Valdivia warmly welcomed Sancho and his confederates, now completely subdued by his own presence and that of the considerable new force of loyal troops under Aguirre, and proceeded to retrace his steps to Atacama the Greater, toward which the whole expedition was now proceeding. On arrival there, he arrested all the conspirators and instituted a Court Martial.

It was a simple matter to prove to everybody's satisfaction the culpability of Sancho de Hoz and his companions. Halters were prepared, and every external show was given to Valdivia's presumed intention to make an end of the disturbance by the summary execution of the leading conspirators. From the evidence of Valdivia's methods in dealing with later troubles of this kind, it is possible to believe that he would ordinarily have had little hesitation in hanging the ringleaders out of hand. He was, however, on the present occasion, faced with the difficulty that the hanging of Sancho might later be attributed to motives of private interest, and thus become a source of considerable danger to himself. To execute the rest of the conspirators while sparing their leader being obviously impossible, he allowed himself to be persuaded by the entreaties of the priests and certain others among the expeditionaries to be content with a less rigorous exercise of his powers of justice. The brothers Guzman and Diego Lopez de Avalos were accordingly sent back to Peru, after the confiscation of their arms and horses. Sancho de Hoz and Antonio de Ulloa, however, were to be allowed to go forward with the expedition in accordance with their own expressed desires and, indeed, entreaties. Sancho himself had every reason to wish to stay where he was, since all that awaited him in Peru was a further period of languishing in a debtors' jail.

Valdivia now began to maneuver toward obtaining Sancho's signature to an act of annulment of their contract. Granted that the time limit of four months from December 28, 1539, had now expired without Sancho's having fulfilled any of his commitments, the fact remained that it was highly desirable to make even more abundantly plain to the soldiery that Sancho would be going forward simply as one of themselves, leaving Valdivia the sole and entirely undisputed leader of the enterprise.

Sancho was accordingly kept in prison during the two months' rest which Valdivia considered necessary in Atacama the Greater for the refreshment of his force after their long and exacting march. It seems probable that informal negotiations were carried on between Sancho's friends and Valdivia's more intimate followers regarding the terms of a settlement. By the use of the pressure of confinement on the one hand, and of hopes of release and preferential treatment on the other, Sancho was eventually induced formally to renounce all participation in the leadership of the expedition. On August 8, 1540, he appended his signature to the now famous deed before the notary, Luis de Cartagena, receiving in return his own release from prison and the written undertaking that he should be reimbursed for the value of some horses and other items of equipment which he had contributed and be "given to eat in accordance with the quality of his person." The latter phrase referred of course to preferential treatment in the distribution of estates and Indian labor in the new settlement. Such were the contents of the first public deed signed in Chile.[5]

The expedition was now ready to resume the march. Once again a long stretch of desert had to be traversed and a hundred difficulties of hunger, thirst, heat by day, and intense cold by night overcome. Those who have lived or traveled in the nitrate pampas will appreciate something of the hardships which the great contrasts of temperature alone must have imposed. Again little is known of the details of the journey beyond the central fact that these men of iron surmounted all their obstacles and finally emerged into the Copiapó valley.

Their hopes of finding rest and abundance here were quickly shattered. The natives of the district, following the example of the inhabitants of Atacama and the presumed injunctions of the Inca sovereign, had withdrawn before the advancing Spaniards with all their available stores of food. From ambushes they constantly harried the invaders and could not be prevented from inflicting considerable losses upon the ill-armed "Pieces." The Spaniards were forced to make foraging expeditions and to fight for the only supplies they could obtain.

Copiapó was the beginning of the territory which Valdivia's commission empowered him to subjugate. It was here that he went through the solemn ceremonies of taking possession of his province in the name of the Spanish monarch. To commemorate the event he called the Copiapó valley, the valley of the *Posesión,* and at the same time christened the whole of his future territory *Nueva Extremadura* or *Nuevo Extremo,* "because the Marquess [Pizarro] hails from there [Extremadura in Spain], and I am his creature."[6] While his attempt to rename the Copiapó valley was no more than an act of commemoration, he had other motives for rechristening his province. Almagro's failure and disappointment, combined with the disrepute into which his followers, contemptuously referred to as "the men from Chile," had fallen in Peru, had surrounded the name "Chile" with unfortunate associations. These Valdivia hoped to wipe out by a simple act of baptism. The maps of the present time are sufficient evidence of the futility of these amiable endeavors.

The numbers of the expedition were now further increased by the arrival of Gonzalo de los Rios and some twenty others whom we last noticed as having separated from Sancho de Hoz prior to his attempt to assassinate Valdivia. This brought the total strength up to 150 men in round numbers, the figure which is mentioned by Valdivia in his correspondence.[7]

In spite of the external difficulties with which these men were surrounded, the spirit of revolt continued to be active among them, centering still upon the figure of Sancho de Hoz. Before the arrival of Gonzalo de los Rios, one of the soldiers, Juan Ruiz, had been heard to reproach Sancho, saying that if the matter rested with him, he would have dealt with Valdivia long ago. This injudicious remark was reported to Valdivia, who immediately instructed Gomez de Don Benito to investigate and take whatever action seemed appropriate. The result was the arrest of Juan Ruiz, followed by his hanging that night.

If Valdivia sought by this swift act of retaliation to discourage Sancho from further plotting, he was singularly unsuccessful. It so happened that just as he had been absent from the camp when Sancho reached it at Atacama the Smaller, so he was away also when Gonzalo de los Rios arrived with the force which included Alonso de Chinchilla. Chinchilla was soon rumored to be making no secret of his intention to kill Valdivia, and Sancho was heard to remark that *his* chief of staff, no other than Chinchilla himself, had now arrived. The promptness and decision of the only woman of the company, Inés de Suarez, averted what might have turned into open rebellion. Acting as though she were in supreme command in Valdivia's absence, she soon had Chinchilla under arrest and maintained in solitary confinement until the leader's return.

In dealing with Chinchilla, Valdivia was again obliged to exercise unusual clemency because of his fears of coming to an open clash with Sancho de Hoz. Chinchilla was allowed to remain with the expedition after simply being offered the chance of returning to Peru. This apparent generosity is probably also partly explained by the cowardice of Chinchilla himself, who, to extricate himself from an awkward position, promised to reveal the full details of Sancho's plot of assassination. In keeping this promise, Chinchilla may have hoped also to ingratiate himself with Valdivia, but if so, he showed a very poor sense of psychology. Previously regarded as a conspirator, he had now branded himself with the ugly stamp of a man who for his own purposes would betray his friends. His ultimate fate had become certain.

After a halt of two months in the Copiapó valley, Valdivia pressed on southward. The Indians fought him all the way down through the valleys of Huasco, Coquimbo, Limarí, Choapa, and La Ligua, and finally he was confronted with the forces of Michimalongo, the principal chieftain of Aconcagua. Time and again this Indian leader reassembled his beaten warriors to bar the Spaniards' path, and it was only after a whole series of sharp encounters that he was finally thrown off. The struggle was taken up by the chieftains Catiputo and Tanjalongo, whose forces also put up a determined show of resistance. The vastly superior arms of the Spaniards inevitably proved decisive, and early in December they finally won through to the banks of the Mapacho to catch their first glimpse of the magnificent setting of the future Santiago, in all the glory of the southern hemisphere's late spring.

5

The Founding
of Santiago

Although no extant document records the exact date of
Valdivia's arrival at the Mapacho, such references as there are
being merely to the month of December (1540), a clue is
afforded by the little hill which the Indians called *Huelen*. The
feast of Santa Lucia is celebrated on December 13th, and it
would seem not illegitimate to suppose that there is more than
just coincidence in the fact that this hill, rising out of the heart
of the Santiago of today and rich in historical traditions, was
renamed Santa Lucia by the Spaniards.

After months of travel through sunbaked desert, broken
only by occasional sparsely inhabited valleys, the expeditionaries now saw stretched before them what must be some of
the finest agricultural country in the world. At this time of the
year the Indian crops would be young and green, the countryside covered in verdure still bright from the spring rains. Had
the leader attempted to calculate the time of his arrival from a
long experience of the country, he could have selected no
better date for the purpose of engendering enthusiasm among
his followers. They were men who for the most part had now
shed, as a result of their experiences in Peru and Bolivia, a
good many of their illusions regarding the making of quick and

easy fortunes. They were, as Encina says, the losers in the American lottery, who were simply looking for a settled life in better and freer conditions than could be found in Spain. Second to Valdivia's own fundamental purpose, the accident of the special psychology of the majority of his followers offers the best explanation of his success.

The first and obvious action was to take stock of the surrounding country. Leaving the baggage in the care of twenty of his horsemen, Valdivia divided the rest of his cavalry into four squadrons to explore the district. The news they brought back was in the highest degree satisfactory. In all directions lay fertile, well watered country supporting a large native population. Here at last it would be possible to distribute large tracts of land, and the labor with which to work them, among at least a part of the adventurers. In such a country even the lowliest soldier might expect eventually to be "given to eat" in the lordliest fashion. So much for the satisfaction of his followers. Valdivia himself, as is abundantly clear from his correspondence, merely regarded Santiago as a steppingstone on the way to the Magellan Straits. Its position as the capital of Chile today had no place in the plans of its founder.

Once the decision had been taken to start a permanent settlement, messages were sent to the neighboring Indians, bidding their chieftains attend a meeting with the Spaniards. Knowing that their crops were still unripe and at the mercy of the invaders, and prompted possibly by feelings of curiosity, the natives kept the appointment. Among them Mariño de Lobera mentions caciques bearing the names of *Vitacura, Colina, Lampa, Butacura (Batuco?), Apoquindo, Talagante,* and *Melipilla,* all of which will have a familiar sound to the Santiago resident of today. Through the medium of interpreters, Valdivia told them that his sovereign had sent him to build a city and that he was resolved to carry these instructions into effect. He drove the point home by explaining that Diego de Almagro, who had received similar instructions but had returned to Peru without carrying them out, had been punished by the loss of his head.

The Indians, hiding their real feelings and intentions, gave assent to what they heard and undertook to assist in building dwellings for the newcomers. The usual ceremonies of taking possession were then proceeded with, including the giving of presents, mutual embraces, and the shooting off of guns. The Spaniards in fact put on every sort of show, says Vicuña Mackenna, that man makes use of when, for the purposes of remorseless deceit, he begins by deceiving himself. A constant reminder of this occasion is now provided by the cannon which is fired on Santa Lucia each day at noon.

Santiago was founded on the 12th February, 1541. The date is preserved by the first entry in the Minute Book of the Municipality, actually written three years afterwards, owing to the burning of the original Minute Book in an Indian attack which came very near to putting an end to the entire enterprise. "On February 12, 1541," reads this entry, "the Most Magnificent Lord Pedro de Valdivia, Lieutenant Governor and Captain General for the Most Illustrious Lord Francisco Pizarro, Governor and Captain General of the provinces of Peru for His Majesty, founded this city in the name of God, and of His blessed mother, and of the Apostle St. James (Santiago). And he gave to it the name of Santiago of *Nuevo*

Extremo, and to this province and its surroundings for so far as it might please His Majesty that this Governorship should extend, the name of *Nueva Extremadura.*"[1]

Valdivia in several of his letters states that the city was founded on February 24, or twelve days after the date mentioned in the Municipal Minute Book. The discrepancy has caused some controversy, though it is now generally agreed that the references are to two distinct ceremonies. The first is the date of the decree ordering the foundation of the city and of the official selection of the site, while the second relates to the setting up of the tree of justice in the main square, the oath of allegiance, and the distribution of plots among the future townsmen. The interval between the two occasions was used by the town surveyor in dividing up the site by means of streets whose size was uniform and fixed by a royal ordinance.[2]

The founding of cities on the new continent was very far from being a haphazard affair. The following extract from the regulations on the subject, issued in 1523 by Charles V, will give some idea of what Pedro de Valdivia had to guide him. "On the sea coast," says King Charles, "let the site be raised, healthy and strong, with due consideration given to the shelter, depth of water and defense of the port, and if possible without having the sea either due south or west; both here and in the interior the site chosen should be vacant and capable of occupation without harm to the Indians or natives, or with their free consent: and when the ground plan is made, let it be divided by line and rule into squares, streets, and plots, starting from the principal plaza and with the thoroughfares leading from there to the gates and principal highways, and having much open country round about so that even with a quickly growing population there may always be room for expansion in a similar manner. See that there be water nearby which can be led to the town, guiding it if possible in such a way that maximum advantage be had of it, and materials necessary for building, and good pasture and arable land, all of which will avoid the work and cost resulting from their being brought from a distance. Do not select sites of too great an altitude, because of the disturbing force of the winds and difficulties of approach and haulage, nor in places too low-lying, because these are wont to be unhealthy; found your cities on sites moderately high which enjoy unsheltered the north and south winds: if hills cannot be avoided let them be to east or west: if a high altitude should prove unavoidable, seek a place free of mists, guarding against ill health and other mischances so far as may be; and in the event of building on the bank of some river, dispose your settlement in such a manner that in rising the sun strike first on the town and later on the water."

Though written long after Pedro de Valdivia's death, and so without effect on the period we are describing, the following amplification issued by Philip II in 1573 is of interest for the purpose of further illustrating the policy of the Spanish Crown in regard to their American settlements. "We order," he writes, "that once it has been decided to settle some province or district under our present obedience, or which may later be discovered, the founders pay attentive consideration to the salubriousness of the site, observing whether the elderly are well preserved there and the young have good complexions, dispositions, and color; whether the animals and herds are healthy and of a fair size and if the produce and food are good and abundant and the earth suitable for sowing and reaping; whether poisonous and harmful things grow there; whether the sky is of a fair and happy constellation, clear and mild, the air pure and mellow, blowing free and uncontaminated; whether the climate is neither excessively hot nor cold (and if a choice has to be made choose the cold); if there is pasture for the raising of cattle, woodland and forest for fuel, materials for houses and buildings, good and abundant water for drinking and irrigation, Indians and natives to whom the Holy Gospel may be taught, this being the chief motive in our purpose; and if it is found that these qualities, or the principal among them, are united, proceed with your foundation, keeping to the rules of this book."[3]

The river Mapacho at this time divided into two channels near what is now the *Plaza Baquedano*. One part continued to follow its present course, while the other flowed down the *Cañada de San Lazaro*, today the important *Alameda Bernardo O'Higgins*, Santiago's largest thoroughfare. The site selected for the foundation was thus almost an island bounded on the north by the Mapacho, the east by the hillock of Santa Lucia, the south by the other branch of the Mapacho, and the west by the *Cañada*, a ravine approximately where the *Avenida Brazil* runs today.

Within this area, Pedro de Gamboa, shortly afterwards appointed the city's first surveyor at a salary of five hundred *Castellanos* a year, traced out 126 blocks or squares divided by streets at regular intervals. The straightness of these streets today is the best proof of the care with which he used his "line and rule" in accordance with the royal precept. Each of these blocks was originally divided into four quarters, each quarter, or *solar*, having fronts on two streets. Every soldier was given his own *solar*, its position depending largely upon his individual importance. It was to be many years before these five hundred-odd *solares* were all occupied. The west side of the principal plaza, the *Plaza de Armas,* was reserved for the first cathedral, the site which a more modern cathedral occupies today. The Governor's residence was on the north side of this plaza, where now stand the post office and the Municipality.

The foundation ceremonies being duly completed, building operations were immediately put in hand. The lightest form of construction was used, the houses consisting merely of wooden frames walled in and roofed over with straw matting. Sufficient Indian labor was forthcoming for the work to be carried forward at a brisk pace.

The next step was the formation of the Town Council or Municipality. Though Valdivia's authority, backed by that of his principal lieutenants, was sufficient to govern a settlement of 150 men on a war footing, he was, nevertheless, merely following normal practice in constituting a municipal authority in a newly founded city. Moreover, Valdivia had other reasons for wishing to delegate a part of his responsibilities. From now on he would be faced with the difficulty of allocating estates to the more deserving of his followers and of deciding between their rival claims to preferential treatment. He would be saved an immense amount of trouble and ill will if such disputes were to be settled by a number of the more distinguished settlers in corporation, instead of by himself in person.

An entry in the Municipal Minute Book dated March 11, 1541, records the appointment of this body. "On Monday, March 7," reads this entry, "the said Lord Pedro de Valdivia, Lieutenant Governor and Captain General, appointed the Mayors, Councilors, Majordomo, and Procurator of the city."[4] The first two mayors-in-ordinary were Francisco de Aguirre and Juan Davalos Jufré; the councilors, Juan Fernandez de Alderete, Juan Bohon, Francisco de Villagra, Don Martin de

Solier, Gaspar de Villarroel, and Jeronimo de Alderete; the majordomo, Antonio Zapata; and the procurator, Antonio de Pastrana.

Such were the beginnings of Chile's present capital: 150 Spaniards building straw huts at the foot of Santa Lucia, surrounded by a numerous and bitterly hostile native population, and having as their only means of communication and support a hazardous and almost untried sea voyage of many weeks' duration or an overland journey of such severity as had taken even themselves nearly a year to accomplish. And they meant not merely to explore and return to civilization; they had come to stay and fight it out. So great was their assurance that they felt capable not merely of dominating their Indian foes and successfully building a new colony, but of indulging in the luxury of quarreling among themselves and intriguing, at the risk of an ignominious death, for leadership and authority in so tremendous and seemingly forlorn an enterprise.

6

The First
Months
of the
Colony

While the natives were still concerned for the successful
gathering of their crops, the peaceful work of constructing the
new city continued to go smoothly forward. With the approach
of winter, however, it was observed that they were withdrawing from the immediate surroundings, and at the same
time displaying a constantly more defiant attitude. The efforts
which Valdivia made to keep on friendly terms were apparently interpreted merely as signs of weakness and failed to do
more than encourage them in their growing insolence.

Once the entire harvest was safely gathered, open threats
began to be conveyed to the Spaniards, and early in May came
the sensational one that the Indians proposed to kill Valdivia
and the whole of his company in the same way as, they alleged,
Francisco Pizarro had just been killed in Peru by Diego de
Almagro the younger. The fact that the Chilean Indians had
news of this event some six weeks before it occurred, Pizarro
being actually assassinated on June 26, demonstrates not
merely the excellence of the communications which existed
between the natives of the two countries, but the notoriety of
the younger Almagro's intention to revenge himself upon his
father's antagonist. The Indians' statement is a little too

accurate, and too near to the date of the actual execution of the plot, to be regarded simply as good guesswork.

The news, sufficiently serious in itself, was of vital importance to the young colony. Valdivia's powers emanated from Pizarro, on whom in consequence he was entirely dependent. Quite apart from the doubtfulness of the validity of such powers after Pizarro's death, it did not seem likely that the Almagro faction, now presumably in power in Peru, would allow the Quartermaster General of Pizarro's army at Las Salinas to retain the office of Lieutenant Governor in Chile. Any new governor, whether appointed by Almagro or by the king, would have his own following to satisfy at the obvious expense of the original colonists. Immediate action was imperative.

On May 10, the Municipal Council, or *Cabildo,* met to consider the situation and instructed the procurator, Antonio Pastrana, to draw up a petition showing reason why Valdivia should be appointed Governor for the King, instead of Lieutenant Governor for Pizarro, pending the Spanish monarch's further pleasure. Two weeks passed without further development, either owing to intentional delay on the part of Pastrana, Valdivia's craftiest enemy, or simply because public interest in the matter died down after the first excitement over the news, which might have had no atom of truth in it, had passed.

On May 29, however, the matter was again brought prominently into the foreground by the confessions extorted from two natives who, by reason of their threatening insolence, were seized and put to the torture. They confirmed that the chieftain Michimalongo had received the news of Pizarro's assassination from the natives of Copiapó, who in their turn had had it from the Atacamanians. They added that the

Copiapó Indians had massacred eighteen Spaniards only shortly before, while this small force was making its way down from
Peru to join Valdivia.

Two days later, the *Cabildo* met to hear the secretary, Luis
de Cartagena, read Pastrana's presentation. It stressed the legal
aspect of the problem. Without mentioning Pizarro's alleged
death, it assumes it, and supposes that Valdivia's powers have
ceased to exist. On the other hand, "the *Cabildo,*" it says, "has
the voice and power of His Majesty, and Your Mercies are that
Corporation and stand in His Majesty's place and have power
to appoint and elect the individual who shall be most suitable
to the Royal service to govern us and keep us in peace."[1]
Nobody, of course, had any claims equal to those of Valdivia,
in the opinion of the procurator, who ends by demanding that
the Corporation elect him as Governor. The *Cabildo* approved
the petition unanimously and proceeded in a body to Valdivia's
house in order to acquaint him with its terms.

Valdivia was evidently awaiting them, though he asked
them the reason of the formal visit. The petition was then read
to him. He listened carefully and requested that a copy be
given to him to enable him to give the matter proper consideration before deciding what should be his answer on a matter of
such great moment to the service of the King and of the
Marquess Don Francisco Pizarro, "my Master."

Valdivia was in an awkward position. No one was more
anxious than he to be free of Pizarro and become directly
dependent upon the king. To take any such step during Pizarro's lifetime, however, was practically to commit suicide.
Pizarro would never forgive him personally, and could kill the
Chilean project by starving it of the reinforcements and stores
which were essential to it. Valdivia had himself appointed the

members of the Municipal Council who were now taking it upon themselves to elect him Governor. It amounted practically to his appointing himself. The crux of the matter was to know whether Pizarro were really dead or not. It is clear that, through the intimacy of his friendship with several members of the *Cabildo*, Valdivia must have been well aware in advance of what was taking place, and could have prevented any representations being made to him had he so desired. The suggestion, however, that he secretly instigated the whole series of events seems to go too far, and it is on the whole probable that, while doing nothing to stem the tide, he took advantage of his friends on the Council both to keep himself well informed and to guide the current into the most convenient channels.

Pastrana, among the foremost of Valdivia's enemies, was also placed in a somewhat ironical situation in having to do whatever was possible to secure Valdivia's appointment. It is, nevertheless, possible to see in his actual methods the traps which Valdivia was so careful to avoid. Valdivia's election by the body he had himself created was one danger. There was also another, that if the *Cabildo* could appoint a governor, they could presumably depose him and appoint another. The precedent might be disastrous to Valdivia in that it would afford Sancho de Hoz the very means by which he might hope to press his claims to the governorship without risking the penalties of unsuccessful rebellion.

Two days later the *Cabildo* met to hear Valdivia's reply. It was a definite refusal. While recognizing the municipal right to take action of this kind in emergencies, he stressed the fact that his own acceptance might still be adversely regarded by the

King and his Council. Furthermore, if the Marquess Pizarro were still alive, he could hardly fail to be bitterly offended by a proceeding which could only be interpreted as being designed to lessen his authority. "But," said Valdivia, "with or without any appointment from the *Cabildo*, I shall not stop serving His Majesty in what I have begun and have in hand, until I die." There is a definite message here to the *Cabildo* that he does not propose to regard any of his powers as emanating from them.

Two days later Pastrana put forward a second petition, but this time on different grounds and in a somewhat different manner. The question of Pizarro's death, and the legal aspect generally, are left on one side, and the whole matter treated as one of expediency. Valdivia must accept the governorship not merely from the *Cabildo* but from the whole colony. Pizarro, even if still alive, might be influenced by those who surrounded him and appoint another lieutenant in Valdivia's stead; in this case Valdivia "would weep with one eye and we with both," for it would undoubtedly entail dispossession and ruin for the original expeditionaries if a new Governor were to appear with an entirely fresh set of obligations. Furthermore, even if there were no change, the rewards granted by a Lieutenant Governor were still subject to confirmation by the Governor, a fact which robbed present tenure of all stability. From every point of view, Valdivia must accept.

The members of the *Cabildo* were in perfect agreement, and again went as a body to call on Valdivia and to demand his acceptance. Once more Valdivia listened carefully and repeated his answer that he would think the matter over and give the reply which in his opinion was most suited to His Majesty's

79

interests. He then told them casually to sit and eat or begone, for it was time.

On June 6, a brief reply from Valdivia was read to the *Cabildo*, in which he again categorically refused to accept the appointment of Governor. Pastrana thereupon declared that he would call the entire colony to an open meeting to inform them of what was going forward. After which, "on the 10th of June of that year the said Antonio de Pastrana, Procurator of the said city, ordered the Town Crier Domingo, a black man, to call the people to council and to ring a small bell which is used for calling to mass in this town, for lack of a bigger, so that at the sound of the bell, as was customary, all the people should come together in a large inn which is just near to the Great Square of this city."[2]

Pastrana's two petitions and Valdivia's answers were read out to the assembly, together with a further explanation of the pressing need of Valdivia's accepting the appointment of Governor. All heartily agreed to the proposition. Pastrana's petition was excellent. The Lieutenant Governor's excuses were worthless. It was abundantly evident to all that Valdivia must put aside his fears and accept the governorship. Not merely the *Cabildo*, but the whole colony now demanded it.

Ninety men signed the Minutes, those who could write deputizing for those who could not. Notable absentees from the list are Sancho de Hoz, who might have been away, and his servant and intimate, Juan Romero. Next day Pastrana read a third petition to Valdivia, again in public when the entire colony were gathered in the Great Square, or Plaza, after mass. Again Valdivia repeated his lines: "I will see, and make that reply which is most in the interests of His Majesty." His listeners, probably sceptical of his sincerity and wishing to force him to an affirmative decision, proceeded to raise him up and hold him aloft, calling him Governor Elect in His Majesty's name.

Valdivia was quick to let it be known that he was in no humor for an exhibition of this kind. Shaking himself free from his enthusiastic supporters, he bade them pursue the matter no further, for "the bay has one idea, and he who saddles him quite another." Entering his house, he repeated that he would give his answer in due time.

The people, however, had now been worked up into a state of mind where they were determined to have an independent governor for the protection of their own interests. It will probably never be entirely clear how far Valdivia was himself responsible, or how far he was the victim of a spontaneous conviction. Whichever of the alternatives was nearer the truth, there was now no avoiding the issue. It began to be insinuated that if Valdivia had no taste for the appointment, there were others who had and were fully prepared to undertake a thing so necessary to the King's service and the public weal. The danger being communicated to Valdivia by his friends, he appears immediately to have come to a final decision. Emerging from his house again, he bade as many as could to be seated and gave his answer.

"Gentlemen," he said, "you are already aware of the demands which you have made that I accept the post of Governor Elect and Captain General for Your Mercies in the name of His Majesty, so that in his Royal name I should govern you and maintain his justice until such time as the facts are made known to him, and he shall make that provision which shall best serve his interests. Your Mercies have seen my replies and, heeding them not, you put it to me that in accepting what you ask I serve His Majesty better than by refusing. And because I believe that is so, since Your Mercies all say so with one voice and I alone say the contrary, it may be that I am in error. And although I might be right, yet it is better to be wrong with everyone else, and how much more so when their point of view is good, having the sanction of the saying that the voice of the people is the voice of God. And because there is no man of learning here who can give me counsel and tell me what is most suitable to His Majesty's interests in this case, where I have no wish to be mistaken, under the protest which I now lodge, swept out of my poor judgment and from the study of arms in which, and not in letters, I have made my career, I declare: that under this protest which Your Mercies shall accept I agree to receive the appointment of Governor Elect for the *Cabildo,* the Judiciary, the Military, and all the people of this city of Santiago of Nuevo Extremo in the name of His Majesty, and so I will entitle myself, until such time as His Majesty send other commands, the better to serve our Prince, King, and Natural Lord, and in no other manner, and to give pleasure to Your Mercies, Judicial and Military authorities, and to all the other chivalrous gentlemen who are here present and who desire and have so much begged me to do what I do."[3]

Valdivia then presented to the notary his protest at having to accept against his will for the exclusive purpose of better serving the King and the Marquess Pizarro, "my Master, whose lieutenant I am." Recognized as Governor of Chile, he immediately had prepared by the notary an authorized copy of the official record of all that had taken place, presumably for his own safekeeping. The poor, weak judgement of the man of arms, not of letters, is conspicuous only by its absence.

On July 20, or just over a month later, Valdivia appointed Alonso de Monroy his lieutenant governor, the most convincing proof that he could give of having himself accepted the governorship. Eight days later he nominated the first Chilean Royal Officials, Jeronimo de Alderete as Treasurer, Francisco de Arteaga as Controller, Juan Fernandez de Alderete as Overseer, and Francisco de Aguirre as Commissioner.

The newly made Governor had done much since he had left Cuzco nearly eighteen months before. But more, much more, was still to do. Without reinforcements and fresh supplies from Peru, the expedition was doomed to failure. Communications had to be opened. By land, a moderate force, besides most dangerously reducing the present numbers of the expedition, would have small chance of getting safely through. The sea seemed to offer the best and safest route, and since he had no ship, Valdivia decided in the most matter of fact manner that one would have to be built.

A ship, however, in itself would offer no inducement to merchants to send their wares southward nor to recruits to offer their services in a country still suffering from the stigma given to it by the results of the Almagro expedition. There was only one argument capable of really convincing the average adventurer: gold, and in abundance, must quickly be discovered.

Meanwhile, the natives were gathering on all sides for a massed attack, by means of which they presumably hoped to exterminate the invaders before they could become more firmly entrenched or be reinforced by fresh recruits. A number of small sorties had already been made by the Spaniards to break up the gatherings, but these had had only a limited and temporary success. Finally Valdivia despatched Gomez de Don

Benito to the river Cachapoal (Rancagua), where he encamped with a body of horsemen committed to the joint tasks
of spoiling and reconnaissance.

The greater danger, however, was northward, and this
Valdivia himself took in hand. Michimalongo was still active in
the Aconcagua valley, and Valdivia determined to make an end
of this menace. The native chieftain had made his camp into a
strong fortress, and it was here that the Spaniards attacked
him. After an extremely sharp and hard fought encounter,
Michimalongo himself was captured, together with several of
the lesser chieftains.

Far from killing or maltreating his prisoners, Valdivia
adopted the politic attitude of showing them great kindness.
His motives were the help which these men could lend him in
bringing the natives under control, and the fact that Chile had
regularly sent a large gold tribute each year to the Incas.
Michimalongo, if anyone, must know where this had been
obtained.

Before giving an answer to the direct question addressed to
him on the latter point, Michimalongo consulted his fellow
captives. They apparently decided that some advantage was to
be obtained in giving the information and delighted the
Spaniards by offering to show them the mines, which lay at no
great distance from where they were situated. Marga-Marga
was soon reached, and, says Mariño de Lobera, "It is impossible to express the joy and contentment of the Spaniards when
they saw the tools; and, as though they already had the gold in
bags . . . they began to grow conceited and self-important in
great measure and to have more ambitious ideas, like rich
people, believing that in a short time they would go to Spain to

found entailed estates, even earldoms, and castles of gold, beginning of course by making them out of wind."[4]

In return for their freedom, the Indian chieftains agreed to provide twelve hundred male and five hundred female laborers for the mines. Valdivia accepted the men but refused to allow women to engage in this work. It need cause us no surprise that two expert miners were readily available from among the expeditionaries. They were immediately put in charge and soon had production well under way. Valdivia was obliged to keep the mine under protection, and for this purpose stationed nearby a company of fifteen men under Gonzalo de los Rios.

So much for the gold. The ship was still to build. Concón was finally selected as the site for this enterprise by reason of its quiet beach, its abundance of timber, and its proximity to Marga-Marga. It is difficult to resist a feeling of amazement that within a few weeks a splendid vessel, capable of sailing to Peru, was well on the way to completion. Master shipwrights, together with all the necessary materials and tools, could be produced with the same facility as expert gold-mining engineers. Any incredulity we may be tempted to feel quickly gives way before the facts. There can be no doubt whatever that the vessel would have sailed and safely reached her destination, with plenty of gold stowed aboard her, had it not been for a serious miscalculation of the native mentality and his capacity for fighting back.

Early in August, Valdivia was in Concón, supervising the final touches which were being given to the ship. News reached him from Alonso de Monroy that there was a conspiracy on foot among certain of the Spaniards in Santiago to assassinate him, to take possession of the gold and of the ship, and to abandon the country. Valdivia lost no time in riding for the capital, with an escort of six men. Intending to remain for only two or three days, he delayed six or seven without taking any definite action. It was enough to lose him his ship and the lives of thirteen Spaniards.

There is some discrepancy regarding the details of the disaster, but we believe that nothing is lost by following Gongora Marmolejo, who at all events gives the completest account. He traces the whole incident to the cunning and treachery of the Indians, and asserts that Valdivia failed to enlarge on the details because of the unwelcome knowledge that he himself was the first to be deceived.

According to this account, Valdivia had been promised a complete drum of gold, and had instructed Gonzalo de los Rios to receive it on his behalf. On the day fixed by the natives, their chieftain approached Rios and handing him several nuggets said, "Accept this gold, and be assured that in a short time we shall give you in metal such as this all that we promised to Pedro de Valdivia." Rios unsuspectingly took the gift to examine it, and while absorbed in the agreeable task had his sword drawn from its scabbard by the wily native, who proceeded to attack him with it. A large force of Indians then sprang from ambush and, apparently taking the Spaniards unawares and completely unarmed, soon made an end of them with arrows and spear thrusts. Thirteen Spaniards, some black slaves, and many friendly Indians, whose numbers as usual are not mentioned, were slaughtered. Gonzalo de los Rios himself and a negro named Juan Valiente were the only survivors. They rode at all speed to Santiago with the disastrous news.

We may well imagine the stunning effect that the tidings would have upon the colony. The vessel, so recently the source of high hope by reason of the prospects which it opened up of establishing communications with Peru, was a mass of smoldering timber. Far from improving the Spaniards' lot, it had actually lost them nearly a tenth of their number. Valdivia set out instantly with forty horsemen. Perhaps there had been exaggeration. Something might after all be retrieved. The sight that met his eyes at the end of his journey undeceived him. The disaster was in every way as complete as Gonzalo de los Rios had described it.

Valdivia felt himself in insufficient force to carry out a punitive expedition. He was also in some anxiety regarding the attack which was constantly threatening Santiago. He perforce returned to the capital, though not before managing to capture a chieftain called Atangalongo and to gather together a number of the dead Spaniards' Indian servants, who had become dispersed as a result of the attack.

During his recent fatal stay in Santiago, Valdivia had been unable to secure sufficient evidence to prove anything against the conspirators who had been denounced to him by Alonso de Monroy. The disaster at Concón at least had the result of putting the necessary evidence in his hands.

His enemies, though their schemes had now been brought to nothing by the burning of the ship, were nevertheless delighted by anything in the nature of a setback to Valdivia's plans as a whole. The less successful the expedition, they argued, the nearer was the time when they could return to Peru. Alonso de Chinchilla, unable to conceal his satisfaction, gave vent to his feelings by running round the plaza waving a martingale adorned with bells.[5] This exhibition, an affront to the whole colony, who had just lost thirteen valuable lives, led to his immediate arrest. There still being no prison, he was

lodged in the dwelling of Juan Gomez de Almagro, the chief
constable, who had instructions to see that he was shut off
from all outside communication, particularly with his father-in-
law, Antonio de Pastrana. Since his food was supplied by this
relative, a particular watch was kept to see that no advantage
was taken of the opportunities thus presented for the passing of
messages.

Gomez's vigilance in respect to the food was quickly
rewarded. Inside a piece of bread he discovered a note, which
he extracted in Chinchilla's presence. No sooner had he read it
than Chinchilla, leaping at him, snatched it away and swal-
lowed it, an action in itself sufficient to point to his guilt.
Though the text was thus lost, rumor had it that the contents
read, "Do not confess, for nothing is known."

Valdivia took a serious view of the incident and handed the
matter over to Alonso de Monroy, "who understood" the
methods to be used to make Chinchilla confess. Torture was
undoubtedly resorted to in his case as well as in that of
Bartolomé Marqués, the next man to be arrested, and in a
matter of hours Pero Sancho de Hoz, Don Martin de Solier,
Antonio Pastrana, Martin Ortuño, and Sebastian Valquez
were all under lock and key. Valdivia's previous hesitation in
taking action may well be explained by the importance of the
men concerned, two being none other than his own nominees
on the *Cabildo*.

Once he had decided to act, however, all signs of hesitation
vanished. In two days the prisoners, with the exception of
Sancho de Hoz, were condemned, and in two days more the
sentences were executed. Chinchilla was the first, being
hanged in full view on Santa Lucia. Next came Martin Ortuño,
who was hanged in the plaza the same day. Pastrana and

Marqués were both hanged on the day following, also in the plaza. Don Martin de Solier, exercising the privilege of his birth, was beheaded. He died on the same day as Chinchilla and Ortuño. Sebastian Vasquez received a reprieve at the eleventh hour, when he had actually made what he believed to be his last confession.

Valdivia must have felt the situation to be desperate indeed. He had just lost thirteen of his small force at the hands of his enemies, and yet he had himself to put an end to the lives of five more valuable fighting men. In his letter to Charles V dated September 4, 1545, he says, "I found many guilty but by reason of the necessity in which I stood I hanged five that were at the head of it and made pretence with the rest." For his swift action he is nowhere blamed, even by his worst enemies. It was still clear to everybody that the long processes of civil courts had no place in what, despite all the pathetic trappings with which the semblance of a city was being built, was a military camp, a camp moreover surrounded by the enemy. The right name for the conspiracy was mutiny, and summary execution was the proper, and indeed the only possible, answer. Confronted by fierce enemies without, and by men whom he suspected and in some cases knew to be traitorous conspirators within, Valdivia carried out executions on a generous scale, "made pretence" where necessary, but remained entirely unshaken in his determination to stay and build a new country.

The minutes of the *Cabildo* during this period make interesting reading, because of their negativeness. On August 7th, immediately before the arrests, the Corporation had met on routine business. The name of Don Martin de Solier figures among those present. The next meeting took place on August 11th, after all the executions had been carried out. Don Martin de Solier is not even mentioned. Antonio de Pastrana, however, had occupied the post of Procurator, a post which could not be left vacant. The *Cabildo* proceeded to replace him. "Whereas Antonio de Pastrana," read the minutes, "now deceased, was named Procurator of this city, and by reason of his death there is need to name a successor in the office; and since Bartolomé Flores, neighbor of this city, is a person of experience, etc. . . . he is named Procurator." No mention of Pastrana's treachery, the King's Justice, the pleasure of the King's Governor, but just the simple epithet "deceased." It is difficult to decide whether these men were stunned by the recent events or simply regarded them as a part of their daily routine. Whatever it is that lies hidden from our understanding behind the bald wording, it is certainly nothing which could have brought much warmth to the stout heart of the leader.

Once again Pero Sancho de Hoz had escaped with his life, but on this occasion his friends forfeited theirs. There is no doubt of his complicity in the minds of the vast majority of the witnesses who were to testify years later at Francisco de Villagra's trial. But Valdivia feared still to proceed against him and again yielded to the entreaties of his own followers, including Inés de Suarez herself, to spare his life. He had good cause to congratulate himself upon his judgment a few years later, when he had himself to stand trial in Peru. Had he then found himself in the position of having executed Sancho, even on the strong evidence now before him, he would almost certainly have forfeited his Chilean governorship, and possibly even his life. The hardness of the head of the "man of arms, not of letters" was in every way as reliable as the stoutness of his heart.

7

The
Lean
Years

While the Spaniards, not content with fighting the natives, were still busily engaged in reducing their own numbers by internal strife, their enemies were gathering fresh energies. The unpunished loss of thirteen lives at Concón and the execution of five of their number by the Spaniards themselves were sufficient evidence of weakness to encourage the most cautious of the native commanders. The country from Choapa to Cachapoal was ready to rise and crush the handful of adventurers who had dared to set foot there.

In the belief that the greater danger lay to the south, Valdivia decided to go himself as far as the river Cachapoal in order to disperse the large force of Indians reported to be gathering there. He took with him a force which he alleges to have been composed of ninety men, but which actually must have been slightly less, and soon joined Pero Gomez, who had previously been posted to the area. Alonso de Monroy was left in charge in Santiago with the remaining forces, consisting of thirty-two cavalry and eighteen infantry.

The Spaniards' movements had been closely observed by Michimalongo in Aconcagua. He had again taken up arms and judged this to be an exceptionally favorable opportunity for attacking and destroying the center of the enemy's power.

The assault by the combined forces of the Indians around Santiago and from the Aconcagua valley was launched in the early hours of September 11, 1541, and was vigorously sustained by the natives all day. The most conservative accounts give the Indian numbers as being from eight to ten thousand, a figure which may quite reasonably be accurate. Although well prepared to receive the onslaught, the Spaniards were nevertheless forced backward, and it was not long before all they had left to defend was the present site of the *Plaza de Armas*. The rest of the infant town's poor buildings were all set fire to by the Indians and utterly consumed. With them the Spaniards lost the two years' stock of provisions which Valdivia had managed to gather together, and the fowls, pigs, and other domestic livestock which it had been Inés de Suarez's particular care to introduce into the new country.

Two Spaniards were killed, and all were more or less severely wounded, but they fought unceasingly and without rest throughout the entire day. Francisco de Aguirre performed prodigies of valor, his lance having to be cut away from his hand which, when all was over, he was quite unable to unclench.[1] Pero Sancho himself was released from the bonds which had confined him since the failure of his most recent plot and did his full share of fighting with the rest. To say, in fact, that any given man was in the encounter is to say that he fought like a hero.

In spite, however, of all the Spaniards could do, the Indians were not to be driven off, and appeared merely to be incited to greater efforts by the swelling volume of their losses. Inés de Suarez is credited with suggesting the action which eventually induced the natives to call the battle off. The Spaniards still held as captives seven Indian chieftains, and her proposal was that these be killed and their heads thrown among their supporters and followed up by a last desperate cavalry charge.

The suggestion was opposed on the grounds that the killing of these hostages would remove the Spaniards' last hope of being able to bargain with the natives for their own lives. Inés de Suarez insisted that her bold suggeston was the right course of action. The position was such, she argued, that all hope of bargaining was in fact now untenable, and that what remained was simply to fight on to victory or death. She added that it was quite possible that the principal object in the minds of the natives was the rescue of their captive leaders, and that the removal of this incentive might well lead to their abandoning so costly a struggle. Little reflection is needed to appreciate both the desperateness of the gamble and the immense strength of character which lay behind not simply the proposal but the dogged insistence upon the adoption of the plan in the face of all the quite natural opposition to it.

So great was the influence of this woman, who had spent the day tirelessly attending and encouraging the wounded, that the decision to kill the captives was finally taken. Inés herself is believed to have assisted in the executions, on the authority of evidence submitted at Valdivia's trial in Peru by Valdivia himself.[1] The chieftains' heads were thrown among the ranks of the Indian besiegers and were followed immediately by a charge of such of the Spaniards as were still capable of mounting a horse.

The effect was electrical. Apparently panic-stricken by the fearful evidence of the chieftains' deaths, the Indians broke and fled, and so brought to an end the well-nigh fatally disastrous events of September 11.

News was at once sent to Valdivia, who reached Santiago four days later with fourteen soldiers, leaving Pero Gomez to lead back the rest of the force. Concón must have paled into insignificance compared with the spectacle of still smoking ruin and destruction which now met his eyes. Not only had the poor dwellings been consumed, but with them, as he writes to Charles V, "our food and clothing and everything we owned, so that we were left simply with the rags we had for war, the arms we carried, and two small sows and a hog, a hen and a cock, and two handfuls of grain." It was not a great deal, says Errazuriz, with which to found a kingdom.

Though Pedro de Valdivia's letters to Charles V and others provide a large share of the material from which the record of these years is obtained, they were written some time after the events themselves had passed and when the prospects of success were beginning to become far more clearly visible. While giving a vivid picture of difficulties already overcome, they fail to supply us with any of the introspective material which a diary, written in the midst of events, alone could have afforded. A brief review of the situation at this point will perhaps take us as near as we are ever likely to reach towards some insight into so remarkable a character.

The first poor settlement was now a heap of smoldering ruins. Every possession but their arms, horses, and the clothes in which the Spaniards stood had been utterly destroyed, with the symbolic exception of three pigs, a cock and a hen, and two handfuls of grain. The saving of precisely these things by Inés de Suarez, Valdivia's most intimate companion, indicates to a nicety how little doubt existed in her mind as to what would be her protector's reaction to so staggering a setback. Until the pathetic remnants could be reproduced a hundredfold, hunger stared the Spaniards in the face, but it is clear that she quite simply assumed that the reproductive processess were to be put in hand.

The natives had come within an ace of annihilating the colony by direct attack, which might at any time be renewed. Meanwhile, they were in a good position to destroy any crops which could be raised in the immediate surroundings and so use this more indirect means of rendering the Spaniards' plight well-nigh hopeless.

It had seemed at one time almost impossible to raise a force to come to Chile at all. It was hardly probable that fresh recruits could be induced to join the colony now, even if a request for them could be got through to Peru. Far less could they be expected to arrive spontaneously.

The bitter disappointment over the destruction of the vessel at Concón must have weighed upon Valdivia, and hardly less so the certain knowledge that many of the expeditionaries wished for nothing better than to rid themselves of his admittedly heavy hand.

Yet during the next two years we can discover no faltering, nothing but a high determination to surmount every obstacle, combined with a sublime confidence in the eventual outcome, which, by all the rules, should have been extermination.

Desperate as the situation had become as a result of the recent battle, Valdivia was not slow to take such advantage as could be gained from the fact that the Indians had put forth an exhaustive effort and had yet failed in their principal objective. Without fortifications or earthworks of any kind, fifty Spaniards had beaten off as many as two hundred times their number with tremendous slaughter. Sending out parties in all directions, he offered peace to the natives, pointing out the futility of the enormous losses he had been forced to inflict. His messengers ran no risk of attack, since the Indians, as was their custom after battle, were lethargic and pretended that they themselves had had nothing to do with the fighting, but that other Indians, from a long way off, had alone been responsible. Fair quantites of food were demanded and obtained by these parties.

The Aconcagua warriors had still also to be watched, particularly in order to prevent their effecting another juncture with those around Santiago. Valdivia decided, in spite of the risk involved in splitting his forces, to take advantage of the lull in the Mapacho area, where the Indians still thought him sufficiently busy in recovering from the recent attack, to make an expedition with sixty horse to Quillota. The tactical surprise was effective, and the expedition successful.

With the memory of Concón fresh in his mind, Valdivia still decided to leave Rodrigo de Quiroga with a dozen men in Quillota, to build a fort from which sorties could be made to reconnoiter and to break up any native concentrations. Not the least of his motives was a desire to reopen the gold mines and to set his friendly Indians to work in extracting what alone would enable him to obtain further support and supplies from Peru. It was not long before he received the news that the natives of this district were gathering in strength, and he sent Francisco de Villagra with forty horsemen to reinforce Quiroga. The combined detachments had a most successful campaign, destroying the Indian forts and breaking up all their concentrations. Valdivia attached great importance to these results and received the returning men with marked pleasure and satisfaction.

Meanwhile, the two handfuls of grain had been sown in an easily defensible place, each seed receiving as much individual care as if it had been a plant in a well-tended garden. Though sown as late as September, the two handfuls gave a harvest of nearly twenty bushels, enough for a really full sowing the next season. Little, however, could be spared for immediate consumption. The three pigs and the cock and hen were at first treated as little less than sacred. They were to multiply to an extraordinary degree in the next two years.

While first things came first, and measures were thus being primarily taken for the purposes of defense and the procuring of food, it was still clear that without support from Peru, the colony was doomed eventually either to withdrawal or extinction. Communications had somehow to be opened. The idea of building another boat (if indeed all the boatbuilders—the expedition was presumably not made up entirely of master shipwrights—had not been killed in Concón) was not to be entertained. An expedition by land was the only solution, and Valdivia decided to entrust the hazardous commission to Alonso de Monroy at the head of five others.

If Monroy was to have any chance of success, gold alone would give it to him. In such time as it had been possible to work the Marga-Marga mines, some 7,000 *Castellanos'* worth of metal had been extracted. Though it belonged to a number of individuals, it was all surrendered for the common cause, and voluntarily surrendered on this occasion. While Valdivia was later to demonstrate several methods of enforcing contributions, no accusation of this kind was ever preferred against him in connection with this particular levy.

To avoid the carrying of extra weight, and no doubt to make a bigger impression in Peru, the gold was converted into sword hilts for the expedition's members and into stirrups for

their mounts. Drinking cups of the metal were also manu-
factured—princely accouterments indeed for the ambassadors
of so bedraggled a collection of adventurers.[2]

They were accompanied north as far as the river Choapa by
a force under Rodrigo de Quiroga, this being deemed the most
dangerous part of the journey, owing to the activities of the
Aconcagua natives. When the Choapa was reached, they took
leave of their escort and continued their journey alone.

All went well as far as the Copiapó valley. Here, however,
they were attacked, four being killed and Monroy himself and
Pedro de Miranda alone managing to escape with wounds. At
the instance of a renegade Spaniard called Gasco, who had
apparently lived among these Indians since the time of
Almagro's expedition, they were followed and finally captured,
a fact to which in all probability they owed their lives, for they
could hardly otherwise have avoided death from starvation,
especially in their wounded condition.

For three months they were well treated by their captors,
and had by that time recovered sufficiently to plan their
escape. The opportunity was soon provided in the form of a
festival at which all the Indians became intoxicated. Snatching
a dagger from Gasco, Monroy stabbed his captor and host and
forced Gasco, now fully implicated, to fly with Miranda and
himself and guide them northward. After great difficulties and
sufferings, the journey was finally completed, Gasco disap-
pearing after their arrival in Peru and never being heard of
again.

Monroy had completed the first part of his mission by
making his way to Peru, though it had taken him eight long
months to accomplish the journey. It was to be many months
more before any results of his efforts were to be seen by the
desperate men who had entrusted him with his task.

Meanwhile Valdivia and his followers continued to hold out. To protect themselves against further direct attack, they built an adobe wall around a space comprising nine of the city's blocks. Though the *Plaza de Armas* is not specifically mentioned in any extant records, tradition has it that it was the center of this place of resistance, and the name *de Armas* of itself provides some corroboration. The wall was some eight feet in height and over five feet thick, and had a total length of more than two thousand yards. The building of this wall by the Spaniards and their friendly Indians in the face of constant attack was in itself no mean performance, "executed by Your Majesty's vassals," says Valdivia to Charles V, "and I among them, and with our weapons at our sides we worked from the time we began it until it was finished, not resting an hour; and, at the cry of 'Indians!' servants and baggage were taken inside, where were also the few provisions which we had stored, and, while the infantry stood to the defense, we on horse galloped to the open country to fight the Indians and defend our crops." There is a fine racy flavor to many of Valdivia's descriptions.

The Indians had now changed their tactics and were laying siege to the patient defenders. Their plan of campaign was not merely to sow no crops themselves, except in hidden distant places which the Spaniards could not reach even if they dared, but to attempt to destroy also anything sown by the invaders. The siege was not a close one, since the Indians had no fancy to be the continual target for the Spaniards' devastating cavalry charges. They instead lay in hiding all around the city where it was difficult to attack them without leaving the fortress itself open to assault from another quarter, or indeed being cut off from it altogether. The Spaniards lacked the initiative and could merely act as the movements of their foes dictated. "It suited me," says Valdivia, "to have thirty or forty horsemen continually on the move in the fields in winter; and when they had finished their rations, they came in, and out went others. And so we kept at it like ghosts, and the Indians called us *cupais*, the name they give their devils, for at whatever hour they came to look—and they know how to come fighting at night—they found us awake, armed, and if need be on horseback."

To the fatigue and monotony of this constant watching and fighting was added the lack of clothing and food. The defenders had lost everything but what they were wearing at the time of the fire, and what they wearing was turning rapidly into a collection of rags, helped out by the use of skins. To such a state of hunger were they reduced that they were eating wild herbs and bugs. Diego de Velasco has achieved immortality by his vaunted discovery of the nourishing properties of harvest flies.[3] And yet in two years of this kind of suffering, without news of any kind which could encourage the hope of relief, there is no word of insubordination or indeed of any move whatever in contradicition to the leader's determination to stay and see the matter through.

With some justice Valdivia can write to Charles V, "What I have been engaged in since I came to this land, and the Indians rose against me, to further the purpose which I have of perpetuating it to your Majesty, is to have been Governor in Your Royal name with authority over your vassals, and over it, and Captain to encourage them in war and be first in times of danger, for so it was best; father to aid them as I could, and grieve for their toils, helping them like my own sons to overcome them; friend to speak with them; geometrician to plan and poulate; overseer to make channels and distribute water; tiller and laborer at the sowings; head shepherd in the breeding of cattle; and, in short, founder, breeder, defender, conqueror, and discoverer."

So passed the year 1542, with no news whatever of Monroy, who had set out for Peru in January. Month after month of 1543 followed on in the same dull, hopeless, yet dogged and determined manner, when suddenly in September came the long awaited news. A friendly Indian came posting to Valdivia, who was some four leagues from Santiago, with the information that a ship was at anchor in Valparaiso bay. It was just two years since the burning of the infant town, nearly three since the expeditionaries had reached the Mapacho valley, and here was their first reinforcement and contact with the outside world.

Valdivia despatched Francisco de Villagra with a company of horsemen to Valparaiso with all speed. The native had indeed spoken the truth. There lay the vessel, the first tangible result of Monroy's mission.

On his way north, Monroy had met in Arequipa a rich Tarapacá miner named Lucas Martinez, a brother of Valdivia's merchant partner, Francisco Martinez. Lucas and Diego García de Villalon, another of Valdivia's friends, decided to go into partnership in sending a relief cargo to Chile, Lucas supplying a vessel which he took from his mining trade, "whereby he lost no small amount," as Valdivia was later to write to Hernando Pizarro. That he was thereby also to save his head, after being implicated in the rebellion of Gonzalo Pizarro, was a credit which still lay in the future. He also put up some 12,000 *Castellanos* in arms and equipment, the rest of the capital being supplied by Garcia de Villalon, who bought a share in the vessel, and Lucas' son, Francisco Martinez, who invested everything he possessed in the venture.

101

In spite of all his friends' protests and warnings regarding the danger of the enterprise, Villalon put to sea without either himself, the mate, or the first officer of the vessel knowing anything whatever of the essentials of navigation. In these circumstances they had no alternative but to come the whole way down in sight of the coast, thereby meeting the full force of wind and current and immeasurably lengthening the journey. They passed Valparaiso without recognizing it and actually reached as far south as the future Concepción before retracing their steps, convinced that they had gone too far. They would again have passed Valparaiso in a northerly direction had they not been sighted by an Indian, possibly placed there by Valdivia for the purpose, who lit a beacon fire which they rightly assumed to be a signal. Francisco de Villagra soon had the ship safely moored in the bay and her cargo on the way to Santiago. Valued at some 26,000 *Castellanos,* more than 70,000 were paid for it. The venture had been speculative, but the rewards were not disproportionate to the risk.

Among the few passengers to arrive on the vessel was Francisco Martinez, Valdivia's partner, who had come to investigate how the enterprise, to half the profits of which he was entitled, was progressing. It took him but a very short time to see what a desperate state the colony was in. So far from there being any profits, the Governor was hopelessly sunk in debt and clearly intending to sink still further, without there being the slightest indication of how he was finally to extricate himself. For Martinez to prolong his association with such a concern appeared merely to spell his certain ruin.

He accordingly appealed to the two mayors-in-ordinary to put an end to so unpromising a partnership, demanding that the Governor return him his original investment of nearly

10,000 *Castellanos*. With some justification, Valdivia saw no reason why his partner should be so easily relieved of his obligations, and accordingly we find Jeronimo de Alderete appearing for the Governor the next day, not merely refusing any dissolution of the partnership, but demanding immediate payment by Martinez of half the expenses so far incurred, which were stated to be 220,000 *Castellanos*.

Valdivia knew the strength of his position and had no intention of paying now the exorbitant prices originally charged by Martinez for the merchandise which he contributed to the expedition in its desperate beginnings. He accordingly refused to give way until Martinez had agreed to accept only 5,000 *Castellanos*, or not much more than half the nominal amount of his original investment, in return for the dissolution of the partnership. The man of arms, it will be observed, was not above the driving of the hardest type of commercial bargain.[4]

Meanwhile, Alonso de Monroy was finally carrying out the other objects of his mission. He had arrived in Peru at a singularly inopportune moment. The country was engaged in a civil war as a result of the rising of Almagro's partisans under his son, Diego de Almagro the younger, and their assassination of Francisco Pizarro. Almagro held the south of the country, and Monroy was fully alive to the danger of falling into his hands. He accordingly crossed the Andes and went to Porco, where he and Valdivia had friends. His only success here was a loan of 5,000 *Castellanos* from a priest, Gonzalo Yañez, who also undertook to accompany him back to Chile. Not long afterward, however, the battle of Chupas put an end to Almagro's pretensions and placed the whole of Peru under the jurisdiction of the King's emissary, Vaca de Castro.

Monroy lost no time in setting out to see Vaca de Castro,

only to be met with a very lukewarm reception when he arrived. Castro was far too busy with immediate concerns in Peru to have any great interest in Chile. From Monroy's account of how matters had stood when he had himself left the country more than a year previously, Vaca de Castro appears, not unreasonably, to have regarded the venture as doomed to failure in any case. He could hardly be expected actively to encourage the sending of further forces to be risked in so desperate an enterprise. Giving no direct support whatever, he could be prevailed upon only to authorize Monroy to raise what forces he could on his own, at the same time confirming Valdivia's appointment as Lieutenant Governor, dependent now upon himself. This appointment was to devolve upon Monroy in the event of Valdivia's death. There is strong evidence for both these provisions having actually reached Valdivia's hands, though, at his trial, he denies having received at all events the first. If he did receive it, he certainly disregarded it, and continued to sign himself as Governor Elect.

Nothing discouraged by Vaca de Castro's halfheartedness, Monroy set about raising a force of recruits and had the good fortune to obtain the enthusiastic backing of Cristobal de Escobar, who furnished 5,000 *Castellanos* in addition to volunteering to accompany Monroy back to Chile together with his son. It was finally at the head of seventy men, with Escobar as chief of staff, that Monroy set out, and after what seems to have been a fairly uneventful journey, reached Santiago on December 20, 1543.

8

The
Turning
of the
Tide

With the arrival of the seventy new recruits under Monroy, the whole outlook changed. The reinforcement gave the Spaniards the initiative, at all events locally, a fact which the Indians themselves acknowledged by withdrawing southward from the outskirts of Santiago. At last the would-be Governor of a vast territory, and the followers among whom he had so grandiosely divided it, would be able to inspect at least some part of what they claimed to be their possessions and no longer be forced to rely entirely on such information as their so-called subjects chose to give them.

Though the natives had withdrawn southward from Santiago, they were still in considerable force and full of fight. They sent Valdivia a taunting message, inviting him to attack them with his reinforcements, since, they declared, they desired to see if the new men were brave, and if they found them so, then they would give up the struggle and submit. "And so I will," answered Valdivia, and set out with eighty horse and foot.

The Indians were not merely in great force; they had chosen their position admirably. It cost the Spaniards several days of severe fighting to dislodge them and obtain an offer of peace. The offer proved in the event to be no more than a stratagem. The Spaniards incautiously followed the native ambassadors and were led into an ambush from which they barely managed to fight their way out. Valdivia returned to Santiago without pursuing the matter further.

Greatly elated, the natives left their excellent positions and again advanced as far as the Maipo. Valdivia, after resting his men, set out with fifty horse and now severely defeated his opponents on three successive occasions, destroyed all their fortifications and earthworks, and caused them to retreat more than 150 miles to the southern bank of the Maule.

To the north, Michimalongo was continually giving trouble and had finally obliged Pero Gomez to withdraw, probably from the fort in Quillota, to Santiago. Later in the summer, Valdivia faced this situation in person and finally succeeded in forcing the continually retreating Michimalongo to a pitched battle in the Limarí valley. The crafty chieftain had chosen a narrow gorge in which to resist. The fight was a sharp one, numbers of Spaniards being wounded before the natives were finally routed. Michimalongo himself escaped, but all immediate danger from this quarter was temporarily averted.

Valdivia's thoughts were now turned toward the founding of a permanent settlement on the way north to Copiapó, in order to secure the route by which regular communications could be maintained with Peru. The matter was brought sharply to his mind by a disaster which occurred in April of this year, 1544.

Four or five adventurers had fitted out a vessel in Peru with the object of sending stores to Chile, the profits to be earned in this way being as handsome as the risks were formidable. Putting in at Copiapó to renew their water supplies, the captain and most of the crew were murdered by the natives, only three Spaniards and a Negro managing to escape. These four contrived to sail the boat southward and eventually reached the opening of the river Maule, where some Indians invited them by signs to come ashore. Their experience in Copiapó made this seem inadvisable, and they continued their way southward.

News of the ship was brought by some natives to Francisco de Villagra who, on communicating it to Valdivia, received instructions to go in pursuit. By the ill luck of things, bad weather not only wrecked the ship but held up Villagra, who could make only very slow progress across the swollen rivers which lay in his path. He reached the scene of the wreck some five days too late, the natives having killed the sailors, stolen the stores, and burned the vessel.

Mariño de Lobera recounts that the Negro, the first ever seen by these natives, was severely handled. "To prove whether he was really black," he says, "they washed him with scalding water and scraped him with corn cobs, and made other efforts to turn him white; but as there is no lending color to black, he remained as black as his fate, and black it was that brought him to the hands of such inhuman beings who, after all this ill-treatment, put him to a most cruel death."

To provide a reasonably safe halting place both for shipping and for overland traffic with Peru, Valdivia decided to send Juan Bohon north to found a city in the Coquimbo valley. A force of thirty men was considered sufficient for the settling of this little known and sparsely populated territory. "And so that they should set out in good spirits," says Valdivia with admirable frankness, "I settled on them Indian serfs who were never born, to hearten them for the fresh trials to which they were to be subjected after all they had endured down here." In three months Bohon had sufficiently dominated the area to found his city "on the sea coast, in a good port," and it was named La Serena after the land of Valdivia's birth. Constant contact was maintained with the new settlement by means of a small coastal vessel. It was founded, so far as the evidence serves us, in August, 1544.

The winter of this year was exceptionally severe, and in the middle of it, at the end of June, another ship arrived at Valparaiso. It was the *San Pedro,* under the command of Juan Bautista de Pastene, ostensibly owned by Juan Calderon de la Barca, who was on board, but really so by his master, Vaca de Castro, the King's Governor in Peru. Vaca de Castro was using his servant to disguise his own illicit profit-making from the young colony which now officially depended upon him. So bad was the weather that Valdivia was unable to make the journey to Valparaiso until August. Once there, he purchased for 80,000 *Castellanos* merchandise valued at not more than 15,000, for distribution among his supporters.

His principal interest, however, was in Juan Bautista de Pastene himself who, in addition to being a thoroughly honest and reliable man, was also a first-class mariner. He provided in his person the very instrument Valdivia required for pushing exploration along the coast southward, in pursuance of his constant ambition to reach the Magellan Straits before some other nominee of the Spanish Court could anticipate him. Appointing Pastene his lieutenant on the ocean, he instructed him to explore southward in the direction of the Straits, taking possession of the coast as he went. For the expedition, he put at his disposal the *San Pedro,* of which Pastene was himself master, and the *Santiaguillo,* which had been brought down by Garcia de Villalon. To support him were to go Jeronimo de

Alderete, Rodrigo de Quiroga, and Juan de Cardenas, Valdivia's secretary, the latter to provide a record of all that took place on the voyage. All received authority to take possession of the country in the name of the King and his Governor, Pedro de Valdivia.

In the power which Valdivia gave to Pastene, dated September 3, 1544, he officially named Valparaiso as the port which should serve Santiago. "And he delivered to the said Juan Bautista Pastene, his Captain, a standard on which was painted the Imperial coat of arms, and beneath it the coat of arms of the said Governor; and he spoke to him as follows: 'Captain, I deliver into your keeping this standard so that beneath its shade and protection you may serve God and His Majesty and defend and uphold his honor and mine in his name.' "[1]

Pastene set out on September 4 and sailed steadily south for thirteen days. On the 17th of the month, he decided to put in to shore and before dark found a port, just south of the 41st parallel, to which he gave the name of San Pedro. On the following day he disembarked with twelve companions. "And when we reached the shore, upwards of a dozen Indian men and women were close to the water's edge, some with long arrows in their hands, speaking arrogantly in a language we did not understand. We made signs and showed them some beads which induced them to allow us to approach. Coming up to them, we took two men and two women, and four of the soldiers held them by the hand . . . Fully armed, with a dagger in his left hand and his naked sword in his right, Jeronimo de Alderete declared that he claimed and took possession of the land in the persons of those native men and women, and in that of their chieftain, for the Emperor Don Carlos, King of Spain, and in his name on behalf of the Governor Don Pedro de Valdivia, his vassal and subject as were all of us there present, and delivered the following address: 'Notary here present, do you certify in such a manner as shall be credited by His Majesty and the Lords of his High Council and Chanceries of the Indies, how I now in his name and on behalf of Pedro de Valdivia do take and seize tenure, possession and ownership of these natives and of all this land and province, and its surroundings; and if there exist any person or persons who would gainsay me, let them appear before me that I may defend what I do against them in the name of His Majesty and of the said Governor and lose my life upon it; and I request and require of you the Notary, who are here present, that you shall certify this taking possession in such a manner that it remain on record, and I beg you other gentlemen here present to be my witnesses thereto.'

"And to symbolize the said taking possession, he spoke the words thrice, loudly and clearly so that we all heard them, and he cut with his sword a number of branches from several trees, and tore out many plants with his hands, and dug in the earth, and drank from the waters of the river Lepileubo; and cutting two large sticks, we made a cross and placed it on top of a tall tree, and tied it there, and at the foot of the same tree he made many other crosses with his dagger: and all together we sank to our knees and gave thanks to God. Witnesses were the Captain, Juan Bautista Pastene, Rodrigo de Quiroga, etc."[2]

Similar ceremonies were twice carried out on the return journey northward, and Valparaiso was finally regained on September 30.

Francisco de Villagra had also been sent southward in charge of an expedition by land, partly for exploratory purposes, but mainly in order to encourage the return northward of large numbers of natives who had fled from the invaders to join the Araucanians to the south of the Itata. Ground was itself a sterile thing for the Spaniards if the labor to work it were absent. The *Picunches*, by this time almost without hope of ridding their country of the Spaniards, had for their part begun to grow tired of hiding as fugitives and to show themselves ready to prefer personal service and adequate food to the life of vagabonds. Valdivia expresses satisfaction at the results achieved in this respect by the expedition, and put Francisco de Aguirre in charge of the post founded by Villagra on the Itata for the purpose of preventing any further southern migrations taking place.

Valdivia's chief preoccupation, however, was still the obtaining of further reinforcements and supplies from Peru. Gold was necessary both to attract the one and to purchase the other. Reluctant to subject the natives to the punishing work entailed in mining and thus give them reason to flee south again, he employed them in agricultural work and sent his friendly auxiliaries from Peru to obtain the gold. They worked with a will, according to Valdivia's account, and to such good purpose that in the eight or nine months' season they produced some 70,000 *Castellanos*. Stress is also laid on hard personal labor carried out by the Spaniards themselves, who had to carry all the necessary supplies of food to these willing slaves. The amount of gold extracted belonged by no means only to Valdivia but, he says, "Your Majesty's vassals lent what was theirs." What he fails to tell His Majesty is the treatment accorded by the chief vassal to such of the lesser vassals as attempted to refuse to lend what was theirs.

The incidents here referred to were brought up at Val-

111

divia's trial in Lima, and are of interest in throwing further light upon his character. It was apparently his habit to harangue his followers in church after mass, this being a convenient opportunity when they were all gathered together. It was in the church on the present occasion that he made plain the urgency with which he required gold. Warming to his subject, he made no secret of the fact that he would, if necessary, lay hands on such poor vessels as then adorned the altar. Reaching his peroration, he demanded of his listeners all the gold in their possession, warning them that "those who failed to surrender it voluntarily would lose not merely their gold but their skins as well."[3]

Juan Lobo and Pero Gomez, reputed to have the largest liquid assets at the moment, were sufficiently impressed by Valdivia's threats to borrow money from their friends in order to hand it over to the Governor, being literally afraid to say that they lacked what they were thought to possess because they had already used it to pay their debts.

Not everybody was so willing to comply, and little attention was in fact paid by the rest of the company to the Royal officials' attempt to raise a loan of 50,000 *Castellanos*.

No sooner had this general attitude become plain to Valdivia than he quickly put into execution the threats he had uttered in church. He selected three men of whom to make an example, Francisco de Vadileo, Juan de Higueras, and Bartolomé Sanchez, probably because they had the most gold, and without further ado had them thrown into jail. There they were kept head down in the stocks, the orders being that they were to receive neither food nor drink until they were ready to hand over what they possessed. The unfortunate victims were very soon persuaded of the futility of further resistance, their friends assuring them that Valdivia was capable of proceeding to the utmost extremes in order to obtain what he wanted.

This incident is very far from being based simply on the statements of Valdivia's accusers. It is admitted by Valdivia himself in his reply, though he naturally contrives quite considerably to change the complexion of it. He states that the punishment meted out to the three men was not for the fact of their refusal to lend their money, but for the insulting manner in which they referred to the Crown when approached by the King's officials in the normal discharge of their duties. The witnesses for the prosecution, however, are unanimous in stating that the three men were not in fact freed until they had undertaken to hand over their gold, this evidence gathering considerable weight from the fact that the same witnesses are equally unanimous in admitting that the Governor made very prompt repayment from his own share of the new season's production at the mines.

With the help of so powerful an example to encourage them, the rest of His Majesty's vassals had small difficulty in seeing the urgent need of "lending what was theirs."

Three envoys were chosen as the instruments of Valdivia's designs. Alonso de Monroy, who had already given such ample proofs of loyalty and capacity, was to go to Peru with Juan Bautista Pastene, while advantage was to be taken of the journey of Antonio de Ulloa, who had private business to transact in Spain, for messages to be sent from Valdivia to the King. In view of Ulloa's having been involved in Sancho de Hoz's plot to assassinate Valdivia in Atacama the Smaller, it is difficult to understand the trust reposed by the Governor in this man, of whom he writes to the King, "He is held by me and regarded by those who know his good works and character as a gentleman and hidalgo, and so he proved himself in this kingdom in Your Royal service."[4] He was to give proofs of a very different kind before all was done.

The gold was distributed among these three emissaries and two nameless merchants, the latter being deputed to purchase whatever essential stores they could obtain for dispatch to Chile. Valdivia set sail with the party on the *San Pedro,* which put in at La Serena for repairs. A certain type of "bitumen" is mentioned as being obtainable at La Serena, apparently extracted from some plant which grew in the distrct, "like wax" and very suitable for the caulking of vessels. Here Valdivia left the ship and returned overland to Santiago. His letters of September 4, 1545, were signed in La Serena and bear the address of that town.

On his return, Valdivia began actively to engage in preparations for the opening up of the country south. It was now five years since he had reached the Mapacho, but apart from the establishment of the fort on the Itata, nothing had really been achieved beyond the river Maule. After the completion of his preparations and the setting in motion of a new season of work at the gold mines, he finally set out southward on February 11, 1546, with sixty horsemen.

As usual there was no opposition as far as the Maule, but small hostile bands began to appear as the party approached the Itata. Valdivia released all the captives taken in these encounters and sent them to their fellow tribesmen with messages of peace.

The only answer to this gesture was the appearance of a detachment of three hundred warriors, who defied the invaders and made known their confidence in overcoming and killing them. Such a force was obviously no match for sixty well-armed Spaniards, and fiercely though the natives fought, they were eventually put to flight with the loss of fifty dead.

That same night, the Spaniards encamped at a place called Quilacura and, apparently without reconnoitering the countryside, went to their beds, leaving only a small guard consisting of Rodrigo de Quiroga and four others. As a result of this negligence, a powerful native contingent managed to get to close quarters before the alarm could be given, and the Spaniards were hard put to hold their own. Quiroga and his four men fought magnificently to give Valdivia time to organize the main defense. A stiff battle was waged for two hours before the natives were finally driven off after losing two hundred dead. "They killed," says Valdivia, "two of our horses and wounded five or six more and as many Christians." The order of importance is characteristic.

The following day, the Spaniards reached the Bío-Bío and prospected the site of the future city of Concepción. It soon became apparent, however, that they were now running grave risks. Several of their prisoners told them that large numbers of the warriors of Arauco had joined forces with the Indians north of the Bío-Bío and were concentrating for a massed attack, to be launched that same night. A defeat at this stage might well have meant the loss not merely of the expedition but of the entire colony. Valdivia decided to be guided by the entreaties of his men and to withdraw, as unostentatiously as possible.

He accordingly had a number of campfires lighted in the bivouac and then moved quietly out, the fires deceiving the natives, who assumed that the men who had lit them were still there. The Spaniards finally arrived safely back in Santiago after a total absence of about six weeks.

In spite of Valdivia's assertions that this expedition was

purely exploratory, there is little doubt that he had in fact intended to found another city and had been obliged by superior force to abandon this design. The Araucanians proper had struck their first blow at their overconfident enemy.

It was at this time that the growing discontent over the division of the landed estates in the Santiago district came to a head. Valdivia had effected a distribution early in 1542 in order to recompense the most deserving of his followers, but this had been done with next to no knowledge of the country or of the extent of the native population. During the following two years, the original distribution inevitably suffered a number of modifications, and a certain amount of confusion and disorder had resulted. Valdivia had put the matter up to date on January 12, 1544, by publishing a complete summary of all that had taken place till then. While this achieved something, it did not go to the real root of the trouble. There were too many estates for the amount of native labor available.

Bartolomé Flores, procurator of the city, no doubt with the full knowledge and consent not merely of the *Cabildo* but of the Governor himself, presented a petition on July 6, 1546, pointing out that the original distribution had been made with inadequate knowledge, that all the Santiago estates together were worth less than one alone in Peru, and that most of them indeed had no more than a hundred Indians, some only fifty, and others as few even as twenty. Their owners were thus quite unable to "maintain arms and horses in an honorable manner," nor were they in a position to offer appropriate hospitality to other Spaniards who, after the formidable journey from Peru, arrived in a state of complete exhaustion. The only solution, said the Procurator, was to diminish the number of estates in the Santiago area, the dispossessed owners to be compensated by preferential treatment in the distribution of land which would in due course be opened up further south.

The members of the *Cabildo,* being as confident as the Procurator that they would not be among those who would be requiring compensation in the south, most heartily agreed with the petition because "it benefits God's service and His Majesty's, and conduces to the good of the natives and to the survival of this city and kingdom."[5] Of the incidental benefits to themselves, they are, of course, quite unconscious.

In a body the *Cabildo* went straightway to see Pedro de Valdivia, and the ceremony of reading the Procurator's petition was duly proceeded with. It terminated with the Governor's repeating his usual lines that he had heard what was asked and "would do that which appeared to conduce to the service of His Majesty and the welfare of his vassals and of the land, and the survival of the natives."

Whether Valdivia made up his own mind on the matter, as he was later to assert to La Gasca when on trial in Peru, or whether his more intimate associates had also a hand in it, it was not until nineteen days afterward that he made his decision known. The number of estates, and consequently of owners, was reduced from sixty to thirty-two. Nineteen men only were actually dispossessed on this occasion, previous changes having already accounted for nine others. To protect himself against the worst consequences of this decision, the Governor ordered, in the same decree, that none of the dispossessed owners were to communicate with their former native slaves, nor to dare to speak to any one in disparagement of the new owners, under penalty of a fine of five hundred

Castellanos and whatever corporal chastisement might be meted out to them as "mutineers, agitators, and disturbers of the peace."[6]

Promises of redress in the form of new estates in the south provided very cold comfort indeed for the unfortunate losers, whose righteous indignation knew no bounds. They complained loudly that they had been deprived of their property without any form of trial, without being heard, without even being notified. Many of them had audience of the Governor and reproached him bitterly for what had been done, demanding the return of what they claimed to be no more than their own. Valdivia soon recognized that openly expressed discontent on this scale could be not merely a nuisance but a threat to the very existence of the colony. Possessed of absolute authority, and being unaccustomed by now to brook any resistance to his orders, he used methods which were quite simply tyrannical. He collectively forbade the dispossessed men ever to mention the fact of their loss and told them "if they had any rights in the matter, to go and obtain redress from the King."[7]

In private his treatment of the petitioners was even harsher. Diego de Velasco related many years afterwards that when he went to ask the Governor why he had been deprived of his Indians, Valdivia replied, "I have done to you as I have done to others whose Indians I have taken from them. Keep your mouth closed and stop speaking about it, for if you don't, I shall hang you."[8] Antonio Trabajano was similarly threatened with hanging or having his head cut off.

By the use of such methods, Valdivia achieved his immediate object, since nobody dared further to voice his grievances in the matter. Later on a number of claimants manged to obtain orders of restitution from the Royal Audience in Lima, the first being Francisco Martinez. Predictably, however, not one of them succeeded in obtaining physical possession of his estate during Valdivia's lifetime.

There is, of course, no mention of any of this sort of thing in Valdivia's letters. In describing himself to the King as a founder, discoverer, conqueror, and upholder of the realm, he does indeed mention the stern discipline which he maintained, "and yet," he goes on, "they do not hate me but love me." He is clearly unwilling to spoil the picture by allowing His Majesty, or even possibly himself, to be deceived by such of the colonists as were successful in concealing their affection.

The whole of this episode provides at least one of the clues to that for which Valdivia has been greatly criticized, his determination to push forward his conquest before firmly consolidating what he already held. The claims of these erstwhile supporters constituted not merely an embarrassment but a threat to the success of the whole enterprise. Insofar as they were embarrassing, they could be settled as he settled them, by forcible smothering. The solution of this first aspect of the problem, however, was in itself merely an aggravation of the second, since aggrieved supporters, when bullied into silence, could hardly fail to become deadly enemies. There was indeed urgent need for compensation to be forthcoming in the south.

The opportunity presented by this fresh cause for discontent was, of course, eagerly welcomed by Sancho de Hoz, always seeking an opportunity to turn circumstances to his own advantage. Seeing his not unsubstantial minority now swelled by the recently dispossessed estate owners and their friends, and having news, as we shall see, of the probable early arrival of assistance from the treacherous Antonio de Ulloa, he decided to make another attempt on Valdivia's life.

Feigning illness and approaching death, he invited the Governor to visit him and help him in several matters connected with his will. Inés de Suarez declares that Valdivia could not be dissuaded from the visit, in spite of the warnings of his friends. "Nonsense," he is reported to have said, "Pero Sancho is a good man; he has already made two attempts on me. Is he likely to make another? If that were so, I would punish him."[9] In view of the circumstances, the words are curious. It is not impossible to read into them a determination to provide Sancho with yet further rope with which he might this time really hang himself.

The visit was duly made, but the Governor was well covered by his friends. The assassin waiting behind a curtain with a dagger had no opportunity to use it.

The conspiracy, however, had wide ramification, and the measure of Sancho's confidence is the fact of his having dared to make overtures to Pedro de Villagra, a nephew of Francisco de Villagra, to support him. Villagra gave a noncommittal reply and subsequently sought the counsel of Inés de Suarez, who advised him to make no immediate denouncement, but rather to use Sancho's imprudence to obtain further evidence of the extent of his designs.

Villagra accordingly reopened the subject with Sancho and received the highly disquieting information that Sancho had written letters to Peru denouncing Valdivia and was awaiting the arrival of a force which was coming down by sea to place the Governor under arrest. He had in fact, he said, just received the important news that two ships had already arrived on the coast in the north, and he expressed no doubt that

Valdivia would soon be in prison and himself in the governor-ship. Nothing can be more damning to the character of Antonio de Ulloa than these disclosures, the two ships being clearly those which, as we shall see, he had obtained in Peru. It is even clearer that when he left Chile he must already have been in league with Sancho and had the deliberate intention of betraying the Governor, who had entrusted him with his important mission. The messages coming through directly to Sancho from the north are also of interest as showing how eagerly the natives were conniving at the creation of so serious a split in the colony.

On being presented with this further evidence, Valdivia immediately drew up a case against Pero Sancho and had him arrested, with the apparent intention of making an end of him.

Once again, however, he prudently refrained from carrying matters to a conclusion which might always have dangerous consequences for himself. Juan Bohon pleaded for Pero San-cho's life, and Valdivia, probably grateful for the opportunity, graciously acceded. Sancho was banished to Talagante, some twenty miles from Santiago, and barred from visiting the capital. Valdivia disregarded all his friends' criticism of his leniency. He had judged to a nicety the limits of the power which it was wise for him to exert.

Almost a year had now passed since Pastene, Monroy, and Ulloa had sailed for Peru, and Valdivia had received no word from any of them, in spite of Monroy's having actually taken messengers capable of making the return half of the journey in four months. Valdivia once again had cause for anxiety and decided in September, 1546, to send Juan Davalos Jufré with duplicates of the letters entrusted to Ulloa, and a further 60,000 *Castellanos* which he had managed to gather together.

"Every *peso*," he says in his correspondence to Charles V, "cost us a hundred drops of blood and two hundred of sweat," a statement which we can believe even more readily than could the recipient of the letter from which it is taken. The owners of the money, too, would undoubtedly have keenly appreciated the phraseology, had they been aware of it.

After the departure of Jufré, another whole year was to go by before, in October of 1547, the first news of any of his envoys reached the Governor. In that month Pastene suddenly appeared in Coquimbo.

News of his arrival was brought by Juan Bohon, together with a letter from Pastene himself, unable to make further progress by sea owing to the state of his vessel. His letter contained alarming news. Pero Sancho and others had denounced Valdivia in Peru; Antonio Ulloa was a traitor and on his way south to join Sancho and to carry their plot against Valdivia into execution. Let Valdivia look well to the men he could still count on.

The news spread fast, and tremendous indignation was expressed against Pastene for his slanderous implication, not the least, we may venture to guess, by the wavering conspirators themselves. Being unable to repair his ship as quickly as he had thought, and wishing to join Valdivia as soon as possible, Pastene finally followed Bohon overland and arrived when the storm of protest was at its height. Valdivia was forced to intervene on behalf of his Captain General of the Ocean, and he writes in the most spirited fashion of the joy he experienced in seeing this trusted friend once again.

Pastene's news was certainly sensational. The King had appointed Blasco Nuñez de Vela as his Viceroy in Peru, and the latter had straightway imprisoned the Governor, Vaca de

Castro, and installed the Royal Audience. A rising against the new Viceroy under Gonzalo Pizarro had led to the former's imprisonment by the very Royal Audience he had himself created. Nuñez, however, subsequently contrived to escape and to reach Quito, where he sought help from Benalcazar. Gonzalo Pizarro thereupon followed him there, and defeated and killed him.

When Pastene had reached Peru, Gonzalo Pizarro was already in power, and had appointed Lorenzo Aldana, a cousin of Antonio Ulloa, as his lieutenant in Lima. Carvajal, "the Devil of the Andes," Gonzalo Pizarro's terrible right hand, had taken charge of this post in the interim. Carvajal had been a brother-in-arms of Valdivia in Italy and held him in considerable esteem. He now planned to make him a dependent of Pizarro's in accordance with his design of extending Pizarro's influence as far as the Magellan Straits. He was, however, under no illusions regarding Valdivia's ambitions in the same direction, and his problem was to keep Valdivia's wings sufficiently clipped without reaching the point of endangering his friendship.

When Monroy and Ulloa arrived, Carvajal passed them on to Gonzalo Pizarro, Ulloa to apply for authority to proceed to Spain, Monroy to obtain permission to take reinforcements to Chile. Meanwhile, however, he secretly wrote to Pizarro, warning him not to allow any direct communication between Valdivia and the King. "The Captain," he said, "is a great friend of mine, well-known, a good man and unpretentious; but, My Lord, believe that with all these qualities, now that he has tasted the flavor of governorship, he will always wish to retain it rather than cede it to another, though it be St. Peter in Rome himself."[10]

Before he could see Pizarro, Monroy contracted a fatal illness, and died a few days later. Carvajal states in the letter referred to above, "The doctors say it was a kind of plague; I say they killed him, not understanding or knowing how to cure his disease."

There can be little doubt that Ulloa had left Chile with the intention of betraying Valdivia and helping Sancho to the governorship. With the aid of Lorenzo de Aldana and other influential friends, he was now successful in obtaining possession of the money entrusted to Monroy. From that moment he openly dedicated himself in earnest to the purpose of raising an expedition to lead against Valdivia.

He was soon able to fit out two ships and to gather a force consisting of some of the more disorderly supporters of Pizarro, a number of the soldiery who had fought for the Viceroy, and a few of Valdivia's personal enemies.

One of his ships was forcibly taken from him by Alonso de Montemayor, a victim of the battle of Anaquito, who sailed in it to Mexico. With the aid of the other, Ulloa succeeded in reaching Atacama the Smaller with 130 men. Here he made several changes of front, being undecided as to his most profitable course of action. His mind was finally made up for him by the news that La Gasca had arrived from Spain with a commission from the King to put an end to Gonzalo Pizarro's rebellion, that the fleet had already gone over to him and had been followed by Ulloa's own cousin, Lorenzo de Aldana. He accordingly joined Centeno, who had remained loyal to the Crown, fought in Huarina against the still victorious Pizarro, and was one of those who escaped from the disastrous encounter and managed to join La Gasca in Lima.

Before reaching his final decision, Ulloa lost nineteen of his soldiers, who were unwilling to take further part in the civil wars in Peru. Diego de Maldonado obtained authority from Ulloa to lead this party down to Chile, and eventually arrived in Santiago with eight men on November 18, 1547. Nine were killed by the natives of Copiapó, two remained in Coquimbo, and Maldonado himself with the rest, says Valdivia, "looked as if they had recently emerged from the other world" when they reached their destination. The overland journey from Lima to Santiago had in no way ceased to be an extreme test of physical stamina.

Pastene's experiences in Peru during this period had been in the highest degree unfortunate, mainly due to the influence perpetually being exerted against him by Antonio de Ulloa. He finally managed to obtain a vessel in which to make the return journey and, though unlucky enough to be sighted by Ulloa between Tarapacá and Atacama, contrived by superior seamanship to evade his opponent and continue his journey southward. His arrival in Coquimbo and finally in Santiago has already been dealt with.

9

The Death
of
Sancho de Hoz

Though the reinforcements brought down by Maldonado were
few in number, they carried with them news which was of the
greatest comfort to the Governor. The threat of Antonio de
Ulloa's attack was now entirely removed, and La Gasca's
maneuvers were beginning to make the political future of Peru
more clearly discernible. To any but those living in the fever of
events in that country, Gonzalo Pizarro's cause must have
appeared as little short of madness. Valdivia decided that this
was exactly the right opportunity for his going to Peru in
person, placing his services at La Gasca's disposal, and receiving at the hands of the King's envoy both his grateful
thanks and the Chilean Governorship *in proprio*. Valdivia
never erred on the side of underrating himself.

His greatest difficulty was money. After the two remit-
tances of 70,000 and 60,000 *Castellanos* respectively which he
had sent with Monroy and Juan Davalos Jufré, his own
resources were exhausted. Furthermore, his methods of raising
loans had taught his followers the value of secrecy and
encouraged them to find means of more securely concealing
what still remained to them. Force being now unlikely to

produce what was necessary, Valdivia had no scruples about resorting to guile.

He caused Pastene's vessel to be brought down to Valparaiso and gave out that Jeronimo de Alderete would be sailing to Spain to obtain official confirmation of Valdivia's appointment, while Francisco de Villagra would accompany him as far as Peru in order to obtain further reinforcements. Contrary to all his previous practice, he now authorized all those who wished to do so to leave Chile by the same vessel, carrying their gold with them.

Fifteen or sixteen of his followers immediately took advantage of the offer, some in order to go to Spain and settle down on a modest competence, others to purchase goods in Peru for resale in Chile. All disposed of their belongings for whatever they could obtain for them, their object being to take with them as much gold as they could lay hands on.

When the intending travelers had completed their preparations and had seen their gold safely aboard the waiting vessel, Valdivia himself arrived on the scene in Valparaiso and invited them to partake of a farewell lunch which he had prepared for them on shore. During the meal, he spoke to them of all the hardships they had endured and overcome together for so many years. Some of them, he added, would even see His Majesty the King, and he begged them in the course of their interviews not to be unmindful of the services which he, Valdivia, had rendered the Sovereign, while he for his part had written and would write again recommending them to His Majesty's notice.[1] With the plan in mind of what he was about to do, this well-authenticated speech is very nearly incredible.

He finally enjoined them to declare before the notary the amount of gold they were taking away, each man stipulating how much belonged to himself or to others, whose names were also to be clearly stated. This, said Valdivia, would be a means of proving how much gold was produced in Chile and would encourage new recruits to set out for the territory, not merely from Peru but from Spain as well.

While his guests were engaged in effecting their declarations, Valdivia made pretense of taking a stroll, unostentatiously edging nearer and nearer to the beach where a boat awaited him. Suddenly he leaped into the boat with Jeronimo de Alderete, his action being, however, quickly observed by the more alert of his dupes. Suspicion immediately ripening into certainty, all broke desperately into a race for the shore in a frantic endeavor to prevent their late host from sailing away with their gold. They might have saved themselves their pains. A man called Marin was the only one to reach the boat, and he was roughly handled back into the water by the occupants.

The scene on the beach can well be imagined. These deluded men, after years of indescribable toil and suffering, saw themselves defrauded at a moment's notice both of the fruits of their labors and of their confident expectation of the early enjoyment of them. Every vile epithet to which they could lay tongue was unavailingly hurled at the author of their misfortunes.

Once on board, Valdivia ordered Francisco de Villagra to return to the shore and to bring back the inventory of the gold. He for his part made a physical check of the bullion actually stowed away in the vessel, so as to verify the individual declarations made by the owners to the notary.

According to the evidence of Francisco de Villagra at Jeronimo de Alderete's trial, the following conversation took place once Villagra returned on board:

"Are you aware of what I have resolved to do?" asked Valdivia.

"No," replied Villagra.

"Then you should know that on this vessel I have found some eight or ten coffers containing between sixty and seventy thousand *Castellanos*. I intend to sail with them in order to serve His Majesty and to lend my aid to La Gasca, who I am told comes in His Majesty's name to punish Gonzalo Pizarro for his rebellion. And so it will be best for you to remain and for me to go. Do you contrive to repay from your own property and from mine these men whose gold I am taking. And stay you in the name of His Majesty as Governor of this colony."[2]

It is difficult to believe that Francisco de Villagra was in such complete ignorance of the plot that this was his first intimation of his having to take over the control of the colony in Valdivia's absence. Jeronimo de Alderete nevertheless states that he also was entirely ignorant of Valdivia's intentions, to this extent corroborating Villagra's evidence. Valdivia was, however, already dead when the two statements were made, a fact which by putting all possibility of contradiction out of the question robs them of some degree of their reliability.

Formal letters of appointment were then handed to Francisco de Villagra, and other letters addressed to the *Cabildo* for presentation by Juan de Cardenas, Valdivia's secretary. Villagra rode for Santiago the same day, Valdivia being in no doubt of the disturbance which his actions were likely to have created and of the urgent need of his having immediately a loyal and energetic successor in Santiago.

Although Villagra mentions sixty or seventy thousand *Castellanos* as the amount "borrowed" by Valdivia on this occasion, the following anecdote taken from Mariño de Lobera indicates that eighty thousand was the traditionally accepted figure. "It would not be reasonable," says Lobera "to pass over in silence an amusing story of what happened later whereby these 80,000 *Castellanos* became known as Valdivia's eighty thousand goldfish, a name which has persisted until today. It so happened that after a few years, when Chile was populated by many more Spaniards and Valdivia had returned as Governor for the King, a solemn feast was held in the city of Concepción, which had by then been founded, a feast at which the Governor himself was present. To enliven the party, a man called Francisco Camacho was entrusted with delivering a comic speech, as is customary at such affairs, Camacho being a great talker and having the gift of lending spice to whatever he said.

"This good man began his speech, and so pointed were his remarks that all were moved to laughter, and among his other jokes the following was especially relished. Don Pedro de Valdivia, he said, has two claims to the name of Peter: firstly because he received it at his baptism, and secondly because he has done the office of Saint Peter. Do you wish to see this clearly? Then remember that St. Peter spread his net in the sea and with one cast took it out so full of fishes that it broke, and this in spite of his having spent the entire night without catching a single one. Which is exactly what happened to the Governor, for when His Excellency was unable after many years to collect what he wanted, he made a cast in the port of Valparaiso and caught more fishes than Saint Peter himself, and not of different kinds but all of the same kind, for what he caught were eighty thousand goldfish without any effort of his own or of his companions, though at the cost of no little toil on the part of the unfortunates who had spent most of their lives in the water to get them. Camacho continued to enlarge on his theme with such spiciness of wit that not a man but roared with laughter save the Governor, who preferred his fish with rather less salt, nor indeed were they quite as fresh as they had been."[3]

Meanwhile the *Santiago* continued to ride inaccessibly at anchor under the baleful gaze of Valdivia's victims. Gradually the futility of any efforts they could make to defeat Valdivia's purpose was borne in upon them, and in twos and threes they began to abandon the shore and to make their way dejectedly back over the long road to Santiago. All that remained was to swallow their resentment, and to make what efforts they could to obtain repayment from Villagra. A sorry sight they presented, "robbed as though by Frenchmen and dead from hunger," said eyewitnesses who observed their homecoming.

On the following day, December 7, 1547, the *Cabildo* met to receive Francisco de Villagra's credentials. His powers were comprehensive, and it was merely a matter of form to present him with the rod of justice, the symbol of his authority, and declare him Lieutenant Governor and Captain General of the colony. Juan de Cardenas then prepared, for the signatures of the *Cabildo's* members, dispatches which he was to carry back to the vessel and so onwards to Spain.

Assuredly none in the *Cabildo* had any desire to offend Valdivia, and all most willingly signed a favorable account of his proceedings to date. They stressed the necessity of his election as Governor proper and enlarged upon his merits, sacrifices, and great services. They pointed out the dire need which the colony had of him and asked for his definite appointment. They also praised Francisco de Villagra, nor did they forget their own services or requests for appropriate rewards. The King, it is clear, was to be given the right impression to counteract the claims which would be certain to reach him from the less contented elements in the colony.

Outside the doors of the *Cabildo* the colonists waited for news and, while waiting, naturally spread rumors. Speculation and unrest were the order of the day. The opportunity was golden for one man, Sancho de Hoz, and was eagerly seized upon by his servant and close friend, Juan Romero. This extraordinary character, who was apparently never seen without a falcon on his hand, was now destined to close the period of his own life, and indeed of that of Sancho de Hoz also, with a feverish burst of the intrigue so dear to his fainthearted master.

Ordinarily shunned by the majority of the colonists, who were well aware of his constant attempts to further Sancho's cause and of the consequent danger of being seen with him, Romero now became a center for inquiry. Sancho de Hoz was still in banishment in Talagante, but whatever might be in the wind would be known to Juan Romero.

Romero's first act was to send word to his master, bidding him lose no time in returning to Santiago. Without the knowledge even of his servant, Sancho arrived in the capital the same night.

The next day Romero continued his activities, sounding out the greatly enhanced possibilities of successful revolt. The men who had been dispossessed of their estates and now others who had been despoiled of their gold, together with all their friends and the original supporters of Sancho, made a strong nucleus which might easily be turned into an overwhelming majority. There were not wanting those to point out to Romero what he had already been quick to see for himself, that immediate action had every prospect of success.

Receiving news of his master's arrival, he hurried to his house.

"What is up in the land?" asked Sancho.

"The Governor Pedro de Valdivia has gone and has taken all the gold with him."

"And what has been done about that in Mapacho?"

"Francisco de Villagra has been received as Lieutenant Governor and Captain General for His Majesty and the Governor."

"And what is said about that in town?"

"All are hot for revolt and say that if there came a word from the King, not a man but would go out to it."[4]

Romero then recounted his own doings and mentioned the people with whom he had spoken, who were many. The two conspirators felt sufficiently confident to decide upon immediate action. So magnificent an opportunity must not be spoiled by the loss of even a single day. The hour was to be between one and two in the afternoon of the morrow, December 8.

Plans were feverishly made throughout the night for the breaking out of the insurrection and the seeking of those who would lead it. Sancho himself must wait for the triumph to be assured and, Francisco de Villegra once killed, would "appeal to the King"[5] and produce his now somewhat threadbare Royal Commission. He must appear to have had no hand in the rising and to intervene simply for the purpose of preserving order. His title to authority must be cloaked at all events with the appearance of legality, and if possible the *Cabildo*, or at least the mayors-in-ordinary, must receive him as Governor.

The following morning Rodrigo de Araya, the second of the two mayors, was induced by Romero to lend his valuable support, though he limited it to appearing after the revolt had broken out. His part was simply to legalize Sancho's position, being himself a properly constituted authority. When the "King was appealed to," he would examine the pretender's title and pronounce judgment in his favor. Hernan Rodriguez de Monroy was to lead the actual movement at the head of some twenty resolute discontents. The evidence of the complicity of these two men is of the clearest possible kind.

Having achieved so much, Romero divided the rest of the morning between inciting fresh recruits to join him and encouraging those already implicated. At midday Sancho handed to his servant his famous Royal Commission, together with a letter addressed to Hernan Rodriguez de Monroy. The letter mentions Sancho's title to the governorship, the culpable behavior of Valdivia, and the need to remove Valdivia's lieutenant from power. It openly states Sancho's readiness to hasten to any call that should be made and stresses the need for immediate action. The passing of a single night, it says, might gravely prejudice the chances of success.

Rodriguez de Monroy saw the worthlessness of the Commission for the purposes of what they had in hand. Its terms regarding the islands off the coast and the territory south of the Magellan Straits were merely what they had always been, and gained little from Romero's explanation that Sancho's other titles had been destroyed by Valdivia when he had held Sancho prisoner in Atacama the Greater. However, Rodriguez de Monroy cared little enough for documents, and appears only to have demanded them at all in order to make certain that Sancho would on this occasion commit himself to the point where he could no longer withdraw and leave his unfortunate followers to pay the penalties.

Without further loss of time, Rodriguez set off to collect more of his friends for the desperate part he had to play. With Juan Benitez Monje, a recent loser of 8,000 *Castellanos* on the *Santiago*, and Martin de Valencia, a well-known enemy of Valdivia and one of those who had arrived with Diego de Maldonado, he made for the house of the priest Juan Lobo, with whom he was also on intimate terms.

Juan Lobo, as good a man of arms as a preacher and another victim of Valdivia's latest exploit, roundly refused to have anything to do with the matter. By way of settling the issue, it was decided to call in Alonso de Cordoba, lately appointed a member of the *Cabildo* and a friend of both men. Cordoba entirely supported Lobo. He could see no sense or justice, he said, in accepting Francisco de Villagra as governor one day and putting him out the next.

The conspirators had placed themselves in an awkward position. Short of resorting to force, their only course was to attempt to keep ahead of whatever Cordoba and Lobo might now do. They hurriedly left Lobo's house.

Lobo and Cordoba agreed that Villagra must be informed at once. Whatever Cordoba hoped to gain by the action, Lobo's motives were of the purest. He was inspired only by a genuine determination to prevent bloodshed and the disastrous results to the colony which any internal fighting must inevitably produce. Both hastened together to the Lieutenant Governor's house.

Francisco de Villagra was by no means alone. The comings and goings of the morning had escaped neither his attention nor that of his close supporters. The presence in the plaza opposite his house (now the site of the Municipality) of some fifty men of by no means peaceful aspect, ill concealing their coats of mail and other weapons, was sufficient to disturb the calmest of spirits.

Lobo and Cordoba took the Lieutenant Governor aside and told him all that had passed, without however mentioning the names of those from whom they had received their information. When questioned on this point, Lobo refused an answer on the grounds that he was interested in preserving the peace, not in betraying the guilty.

"Tell me who the man is or I'll knife you," said Villagra in high excitement.

"Well you may, sir, in fact," said Lobo, "but not in justice."[6] The coldly spoken words had their effect on the Lieutenant Governor, who in any case had little need to be more fully informed of where the danger lay. Villagra simply bade Lobo go prepare himself and rejoin as soon as possible the small group who had now the duty of defending the public authority by force of arms.

Villagra could no longer doubt the extreme gravity of the situation. He bade the six men who were with him to go and arm as quickly as possible and to return with as many others as they could find who were prepared to support the properly constituted authority. For his own part, he gathered together his own and Valdivia's servants and put on his coat of mail.

He was not long kept waiting. Lobo and Cordoba, shortly after leaving his house, ran into Hernan Rodriguez de Monroy, now extremely uneasy about their meeting earlier in the morning. To Rodriguez's direct question, Lobo unhesitatingly replied that Villagra knew what was on foot and that Rodriguez's best course was an immediate confession, advice which he repeated with even greater insistence upon being shown the letter written to Rodriguez by Sancho de Hoz.

Rodriguez, on finding the worst of his fears so well founded, ceased to feel any scruples over betraying his fellow conspirators if he could thereby save his own neck. He immediately accompanied Cordoba and Lobo back to Villagra's house and informed the Lieutenant Governor of everything he knew.

Though the letter itself damned the recipient almost as completely as the writer, nevertheless its voluntary surrender at such a moment was of immense service. It gave Villagra exactly what he needed for taking immediate and definite action, and he found no difficulty in pardoning Rodriguez for his share in the plot up to that point.

Messages had been sent to all Villagra's sure supporters, who now began to move towards his house. Among them Pedro de Villagra, while on his way to the meeting place, caught sight of Juan Romero, whom, with the aid of Alonso Sanchez, he immediately arrested. Francisco de Villagra, his attention concentrated on the principal conspirator, paid little attention beyond ordering that Romero be thrown into prison, Juan de Almonacid's house being used for the purpose. The detention of this man, the most active link between the conspirators, was nevertheless of the highest importance.

Once Villagra felt himself in sufficient force, he proceeded to follow the advice of Francisco de Aguirre, who, after seeing Sancho's letter, recommended the summary execution of the traitor. The task of arresting him was committed to Juan Gomez de Almagro, the chief constable, and four others including Alonso de Cordoba.

The commission had no trouble in carrying out what might have been an extremely dangerous task, Sancho being in fact found alone in his house and offering no resistance. On being brought before Francisco de Villagra, he cravenly begged to be allowed to speak when a determined cry for support from his partisans might still have succeeded. Knowing that his death must be now nearly certain, and that a cry for rebellion could be his only chance, he meekly obeyed Villagra's stern command to be silent. Not even desperation could lend him the courage for unequivocal action. He allowed himself to be hurried out of the reach of his potential followers by a handful of men who had the enormous advantage of knowing, and showing that they knew, their own minds.

Villagra's house was a poor affair and offered very little security. Aguirre's on the other hand, the only two-storied building then in Santiago and situated on the east side of the plaza on the corner of what are now *Estado* and *Monjitas* streets, was with some reason described by its owner as a fort, and Sancho was hurriedly conducted thither. The doors were then firmly secured and guárded from the outside by Pedro de Villagra and several arquebusiers who had strict injunctions to allow nobody to enter. A quick and audacious attack by the conspirators was still very greatly to be feared.

Swiftly as Villagra now desired to be rid of Sancho, he was equally anxious that there be no doubt of the justice of his own actions. He had accordingly taken the notary Luis de Cart-agena along with him, and once the doors were closed, he had Sancho's hands tied and began to question him in the house's open patio.

"Señor Pero Sancho," he said, "here I have the letter which you wrote today to Hernan Rodriguez de Monroy, signed in your name and by your hand; tell me who are those who were to come to your help."

When Sancho kept silent, not knowing how to reply,

Villagra showed him the letter and went on, "This letter in your hand and with your signature, what did you write it for? Was it to serve the King? And why did you convoke a gathering?"

When Sancho, now mortally afraid, could still find no answer, Villagra continued, "Why do you not answer? This signature and writing are yours, for all of us here present are your friends and recognize them; if they are yours say so, and if not then say that also."

Sancho thereupon acknowledged the letter and added, "Senor Francisco de Villagra, Your Mercy is good and a gentleman; for the love of God do not kill me; throw me on a dester island where I can do penance for my sins, which is just as much death as killing me."

Paying no heed, Villagra went on, "Who are the men of your band? I now want nothing from you but that."

Sancho might have felt the temptation to use this last desperate method of avoiding execution. If he did, he resisted it with a dignity which does a good deal to improve our final estimation of him.

"Sir, Your Mercy is a gentleman; be pleased to behave with me as such."[7]

Villagra was quite unaware of what might by now be going on outside, and was desperately anxious to be rid of the chief conspirator as soon as possible and, by publishing the news of his death, to remove the principal motive for the conspiracy. Having transferred the prisoner to one of the rooms off the patio, he immediately and without hesitation commanded the chief constable to cut off his head. Gomez de Almagro, after insisting on receiving this order in writing, handed his sword to a Negro, who duly executed the sentence.

The first news of what had been happening came to the anxious crowd of men in the Plaza from a soldier called Cordero, who emerged from Aguirre's house crying, "May God forgive him." He was closely followed by the Negro executioner, who carried Sancho's head in his hands, and by others who carried the body. Both were taken to the Tree of Justice in the plaza while the town crier shouted aloud, "This is the Justice ordered to be done by His Majesty and in his Royal name by the magnificent Lord Francisco de Villagra, Lieutenant Governor and Captain General in the name of His Majesty and in that of the very magnificent Lord Pedro de Valdivia, Governor Elect and Captain General in this kingdom of *Nueva Extremadura*, to this man as a traitor and mutineer against His Majesty's Royal service, ordering that his head be cut off therefore that it may serve as a punishment to him and a warning to others. For such crimes such is the payment."[8]

Straightway from Aguirre's house, Villagra set off across the plaza to deal with the lesser conspirator, still lodged in Almonacid's house. The attitude of most of the men in the crowd through which Villagra had to pass was still uncertain, and a false move might yet set alight the blaze of civil war. A number of the rougher elements moved aggressively toward the Lieutenant Governor as he approached, and particularly a certain Francisco de Raudona, a desperate character who openly expressed his hatred of Valdivia, and was eventually to meet his death by execution in Peru.

In a provoking tone and manner, Raudona said to Villagra, as he approached, "My Lord General, what has been done is enough." "Whatever Your Honor commands must be carried out," said Villagra, with great politeness, passing quickly and smoothly forward.[9] Raudona was given no opportunity or time for provoking an incident which could still have had disastrous results.

Juan Romero was soon released from the stocks in which he had thus far been detained, and immediately began a full and sincere confession. As more and more people were mentioned, Villagra finally ordered all but the notary to withdraw in order to restrict as far as possible to himself alone the knowledge of the names of those who were implicated. Finally, stunned himself by the number and quality of the conspirators, he put an end to the dismal recital. "No more, for the love of God," he is said to have exclaimed, and on leaving the house, "There are not eight men in the city but were in it." On meeting Francisco de Aguirre soon afterwards and being questioned, he said, "It has been the devil; there are so many involved in the conspiracy that it is impossible to deal with the matter except by making pretense."[10]

Romero was given a summary trial on overwhelming evidence, and Francisco de Villagra signed the sentence: ". . . I order that the said Juan Romero die for his offense and be taken through the customary streets of this city with a noose around his neck, with a public crier to make known his crime, and that once arrived at the public plaza of this city, he be hanged until he give up his spirit and die naturally, that it may serve as a punishment to him and an example to others . . ."[11]

In the early hours of December 9, Romero was told of the sentence, and before midday he was duly led through the streets with the halter around his neck. When he at last stood on the scaffold, Luis de Cartagena, the notary and only person apart from Villagra who knew the full extent of his confession, tried to induce him at this supreme moment to withdraw the charges he had made against so many. "Romero," he said, "look at where you now stand, and that you are leaving behind you many who have been damned by your confession: look well if it is really so."

Without hesitation the prisoner answered, "From where I stand what I have said is the truth and so may the most glorious Mother of God accompany me on this road which I am to travel."[12]

With those words the ladder was removed, and Juan Romero was hanged.

In a conspiracy which had been so general, Villagra saw the imperative need of issuing a general amnesty and particularly of impressing upon the colonists the scrupulousness with which its terms would be observed. Anything less could only create fear, suspicion, and finally a further outbreak. He accordingly called a public meeting on the afternoon of the day on which Romero died, and made the following speech:

"I have already punished Pero Sancho and Romero, because they had induced some to rebel against the King's service, as Romero related in his confession. And I have no wish to punish these others, for they are many, and because I believe that if they had not been incited thereto by Sancho and Romero they would never have conspired as they did. I pardon them all on the condition that henceforth they serve His Majesty. My firm intention is this, but should any behave otherwise, I will hang him as I have hanged others."[13]

As time passed, Francisco de Villagra's sincerity became manifest, and indeed during the rest of his life the incident was never used by him against any man who had been implicated in it. Villagra had by his courage and resolution done a most signal service to the colony, and hardly a lesser one to Valdivia himself.

It might yet be possible to warn Valdivia of the disturbing events which had just taken place. A messenger was dispatched wih all haste to Quintero, whither Valdivia had gone in the *Santiago* to await Juan de Cardenas' return from Santiago. Cardenas had set out for the coast on the night of December 7 and arrived at midday on the 8th. Valdivia was just preparing to set sail on the 9th when from the vessel was discerned the moving figure of a horseman on the skyline of the coastal range of hills. The Governor awaited the messenger and was soon in possession of the momentous news.

10

Pedro de Valdivia
in
Peru

While we may legitimately conclude that Valdivia felt relief at being finally rid of his old enemy, Sancho de Hoz, without having himself to be directly implicated in his execution, we have in fact no direct evidence of his reaction to the news. What we do know is that the turn of events had no effect upon his plans, and that he appeared to be entirely satisfied that Francisco de Villagra had the situation so well in hand as to make his own return to Santiago unnecessary.

Valdivia sailed from Quintero on December 13 and reached Coquimbo, the port of La Serena, in two days. Here he received the news of the battle of Huarina, related in such a manner as to give the impression that the rebel Gonzalo Pizarro had definitely triumphed over the King's emissary, La Gasca.

Valdivia judged this to be an excellent opportunity for demonstrating the sincerity of his own intentions, and accordingly took steps to let it be known to the *Cabildo* of La Serena that he was on his way to join the loyal forces under La Gasca, the *Cabildo* in their turn passing this news on to the King and to La Gasca himself.

In Tarapacá, which he reached on December 24, the news

was considerably less alraming. La Gasca himself had not been defeated at Huarina, but merely a force of loyalists under Centeno. Furthermore, definite confirmation was forthcoming of the desertion of the fleet from Gonzalo Pizarro, a fact which relieved Valdivia of further anxiety regarding the safety of the remainder of his voyage to Peru. He nevertheless continued to hug the coast and made a number of cautious landings with the object of keeping himself as up-to-date as possible with the tide of events. He finally reached Callao in safety in the middle of January, 1548.

From Lima he wrote to La Gasca, already preparing for his test of armed strength with Pizarro, and asked him to wait for him, since he would require only from eight to ten days to provide himself and his men with the necessary military equipment. When we consider that his whole party consisted of not more than a dozen soldiers, it becomes clear that Valdivia could only mean that it was his personal value as a general, not the strength of his force, which was to make it worthwhile for an army to interrupt its plans for ten days. This pleasant touch of self-assurance lends further color to our picture of him.

After spending a sum of 60,000 *Castellanos* in eight or ten days, some of it on his own party and the balance on others who needed help in order to join the loyalist troops, Valdivia reached La Gasca's forces in the valley of Andahuailas on February 24. There is clear evidence that his value was rated by others nearly as highly as he rated it himself, Diego de Fernandez stating that there was general rejoicing in the army on his arrival and for the excellent reason, according to another anonymous chronicler, that he was regarded by most as the only man in Peru who was a match for Pizarro's commander,

Carvajal. If we are to believe Valdivia's own account, La Gasca welcomed him by stating that he felt more grateful for his arrival in person than for an army of eight hundred men.

Certain it is that he was at once given high authority and admitted to a council consisting of La Gasca himself, who retained the overriding direction of the campaign in his own hands, and of two others, Marshall Alonso de Alvarado and General Pedro de Hinojosa.

From Valdivia's letters, one gathers the quite unmistakable impression that he was the commander-in-chief, entirely responsible for the whole of the loyalist forces at the battle of Jaquijaguana, an impression which may well be a true one if we remember that La Gasca was a priest and neither Hinojosa nor Alvarado outstandingly gifted generals. The strongest confirmation, however, comes from Diego de Fernandez, who quotes Carvajal as saying, when he saw the loyalist forces drawn up opposite him, "Either Valdivia is in the land and marshaling the field, or it's the Devil."[1] If true, the remark offers as remarkable testimony to the military qualities of the speaker as to those of Valdivia himself.

The battle of Jaquijaguana, which took place on April 9, 1548, was little else but a rout. La Gasca had offered a general amnesty to all the rebels who cared to desert, and before any real fighting started, Pizarro's army had literally disintegrated.

Gonzalo Pizarro was soon taken, and Valdivia claims himself to have led Carvajal captive to La Gasca. When Centeno, who had been so severely defeated by Carvajal at Huarina, attempted to be of service to the now 84-year-old "Devil of the Andes" and to keep away some of the soldiery who were only too glad of the opportunity to pay off old scores against a ruthless disciplinarian, Carvajal sarcastically asked to whom he was indebted for the kindness. "Does Your Honor not know me?" asked Centeno. "It is so long since I saw anything of you but your back," replied Carvajal, "that now I look you in the face, I don't recognize you."[2] With the awful death of a traitor staring him in the face, this extraordinary character would make no concessions of politeness even to those who desired to help him in his extremity.

According to his own account, Valdivia addressed the following words to La Gasca, surrounded by three bishops and a number of officers, when all was over:

"Sirs, I am now free of my word and oath, given each day to Your Lordship and Your Honors, and yesterday to the Marshall, that I would break the enemy without the loss of thirty men."

"My Lord Governor," replied La Gasca, "His Majesty indeed owes you much."[3]

The answer seems to contain a touch of tolerant amusement at the boast, especially if we consider that the victory owed little if anything to military superiority and had chiefly been gained by La Gasca's personal sagacity, so clearly demonstrated by his every move since arriving on the continent. If there was any slight sarcasm, Valdivia was supremely unaware of it. His attention was riveted on the opening words of the reply, for this was the first time that La Gasca had addressed him by any title other than Captain. At last his ambition to be officially appointed Governor for the King was to be realized.

Valdivia accompanied La Gasca to Cuzco, and it was there on April 23 that he was formally appointed to the Chilean Governorship, with a stipend of 2,000 *Castellanos* a year. There were, however, limits to his satisfaction, since his desire to have no southern boundary to his territory was frustrated. La Gasca fixed this on the 41st parallel, slightly below where Valdivia was shortly to found the city which today bears his name, and made Copiapó, on the 26th parallel, the northern frontier. These limits were as arbitrary as the hundred leagues (approximately 340 miles) of width given to the territory, measured inland from the irregular Pacific shores and so giving a perfectly impossible eastern boundary well inside what is now the Argentine Republic. So little was securely known, however, of the real natural boundaries that only arbitrary measures of this kind, regarded as provisional, were possible.

Valdivia stayed in Cuzco for about fifteen days and was able in that time to gather together some eighty recruits for Chile. These he sent forward under Esteban de Sosa with the object of their procuring in the Atacama valley the food necessary for other parties of recuits which he planned should forgather there.

From Cuzco he went to Lima and, armed with full authority from La Gasca, purchased three vessels on credit. In spite of difficulties maliciously put in his way by Lorenzo de Aldana, he managed to complete his arrangements for sailing at the end of a month. He himself again disembarked in Pascua with the object of joining another force of ninety men recruited by his envoys and now awaiting him in Arequipa. These he proposed to lead overland to Chile, while Jeronimo de Alderete was left in charge of the expedition proceeding on southward by sea.

In his anxiety to obtain recruits, Valdivia was admitting almost anybody to his ranks, even though La Gasca had forbidden him to take with him any Peruvian natives, who were now becoming scarce, or any refugees from Gonzalo Pizarro's rebel army. Such was the conduct of some of his latest

148

acquisitions that the residents of Arequipa had serious cause for complaint, and Valdivia was forced to leave the town without obtaining further reinforcements there. He consequently decided to march for Chile without further ado.

He was, however, destined to be longer away from his territory than he supposed. Lorenzo de Aldana and Antonio de Ulloa were seeing to it that complaints were reaching La Gasca regarding Valdivia's behavior, and it was probably from the latter that he learnt of the story of Valdivia's responsibility for the execution of Sancho de Hoz, the allegedly rightful governor, and of his being now so detested in Chile that his return there would cause serious disturbances.

La Gasca might have felt justified in shutting an eye to some of the minor complaints, but the suggestion that Valdivia had killed Sancho de Hoz was far too serious to be overlooked and had the special aggravation that La Gasca, in making Valdivia Governor of Chile, might be replacing a rightful governor by none other than the governor's own murderer.

Calling Hinojosa, lately Valdivia's colleague in the high command of the campaign against Pizarro, he commissioned him to follow Valdivia and to try discreetly to ascertain the truth or otherwise of the charges preferred against him, particularly those touching Sancho de Hoz and the bad feeling said to exist in Chile. His excuse was to be the freeing of certain Peruvian Indians whom Valdivia was known to have taken with him, against official instructions, and the arrest of at least one refugee from Pizarro's army, also wrongly recruited by Valdivia. If he thought Valdivia was guilty on the major counts, he was to procure his return. If he appeared innocent, he should be allowed to proceed.

Hinojosa overtook Valdivia in the Sama valley. He soon

149

heard enough to justify, in his own mind, Valdivia's return, and he accordingly invited him to accompany him back to Lima. Valdivia refused this invitation on the grounds that intolerable delay would be caused in his regaining his province and that his forces would inevitably shrink from dispersal if he left them under other command. Hinojosa adds that Valdivia then took the opportunity to parade his men before him, Hinojosa having only nine soldiers in his own escort, in order to demonstrate the futility of any attempt to compel Valdivia by force.

So far Hinojosa had merely made suggestions. He now resolved to make use of his written commission. Early in the morning he posted his musketeers at the door of Valdivia's lodging and, himself entering, presented his orders. La Gasca's wishes being now clear to him, Valdivia wisely made no further demur. He immediately agreed to return, merely reproaching Hinojosa for not having gone straight to the point in the first place. It was agreed that Valdivia's forces should go forward under the command of Francisco de Ulloa. Valdivia himself under Hinojosa's escort reached Lima on October 20.

La Gasca showed every sign of pleasure at Valdivia's action in obeying his summons and paid him the compliment of going personally to meet him on his arrival. Valdivia was allowed complete freedom, and it seems probable that the inquiry would ordinarily have been short and restricted. It became complicated, however, by the astonishingly well-timed arrival from Chile on October 22 of a delegation composed partly of Valdivia's enemies. We must return to events in Santiago to see what had led up to the arrival of this delegation.

Valdivia had left Chile in December, 1547. The latest news from Peru which was known in Santiago considerably predated this event, since it was contained in a letter from La Gasca written on October 15, 1547, and brought down by Juan Davalos Jufré, who took six months to make the journey and arrived in April, 1548. He had, of course unknowingly passed Valdivia somewhere on the way, and since then there had been complete silence.

As month succeeded month without word, anxiety gradually grew keen. The wish being father to the thought, Valdivia's enemies were easily able to interpret the silence in a manner which his friends, ignorant of the favorable outcome of events in Peru, were unable to refute. Finally in August, some of Valdivia's bitterest opponents demanded permission to sail to Peru. This permission was granted by Francisco de Villagra for reasons which are obscure and have led to considerable controversy.

On the face of things, it seemed a poor service for the Governor to be paid by the Lieutenant he had appointed in his stead, and Gongora Marmolejo who, it must be borne in mind, actually served in Chile under Valdivia, is convinced that both in this and in his subsequent actions Villagra is guilty of plotting to obtain the governorship at Valdivia's expense. We can only form our own judgment in the light of the recorded facts.

At a meeting of the *Cabildo* on August 22, a commission was appointed to write a letter to La Gasca in reply to the one brought down by Jufré, This letter was to be delivered by those of Valdivia's enemies who had obtained Villagra's authority to make the journey to Peru. Bernardino de Mella, a friend of Valdivia's, took the occasion to propose that two special emissaries should bear this letter to Peru, armed with the authority not merely of the *Cabildo* but of the entire colony, with the object, should Valdivia be dead, of demanding the appointment of a new Governor. As Errazuriz points out, the suspicion of Valdivia's death must have been deeply rooted in the colony for one of his own friends to make such a proposal, though the concealed object of it may well have been to ensure that envoys favorable to Valdivia should be present in Peru to counteract the accusations of his enemies. The *Cabildo's* response was to name not two but one representative, Pedro de Villagra, first cousin of Francisco de Villagra himself. However innocent the real motives underlying this appointment, it must be admitted that Valdivia's friends had some reason to feel that matters were becoming serious.

They accordingly presented a petition to the *Cabildo* on Valdivia's behalf, demanding that La Gasca be urgently requested to confirm his appointment as Governor. To this the *Cabildo* finally agreed, with the proviso, in the overall interests of the colony, that two letters and not one should be written to La Gasca, the first asking for Valdivia's appointment and the second for that of Villagra. The former of these two documents was to be presented if all was well with Valdivia, the second only if his appointment and return were for any reason to prove impossible.

Gongora Marmolejo takes the gravest view of these two letters and regards them as conclusive evidence of Villagra's duplicity, a view which we believe it is unnecessary to share. In the normal course of events, the first of the two letters only would be presented and would request Valdivia's appointment. Only if it were seen to be impossible for Valdivia to return, for whatever reason, was the second letter asking for Villagra's appointment to be used. Granted that we can assume that Villagra would wish to be governor, there is nothing in any of his actions either at this time or any other during his career which necessarily implies disloyalty to Valdivia, who would, in similar circumstances to those in which Villagra now found himself placed, have been the first to approve the course which was being adopted. The second letter, if used as provided (and it would obviously have been highly dangerous to use it otherwise) was merely a matter of ordinary prudence in ensuring the rapid appointment of an alternative governor, an appointment of which the colony stood in urgent need. "Of intention," sums up Errazuriz, "we are ignorant: the facts condemn no one."

On balance we must agree with this view, even when we wonder, as Errazuriz did not, why the contents of the two letters were not condensed into one. The opportunity for maneuver placed in the hands of the envoy by a choice of two documents cannot but give rise to uneasy conjecture as to intentions of which, and here Errazuriz is entirely right, we have no conclusive evidence in either direction.

Pedro de Villagra, the official delegate, accompanied by a number of others including some of Valdivia's enemies, sailed on September 29 and reached Lima on October 22, two days after Valdivia himself.

Valdivia's opponents could hardly fail to feel that matters were playing into their hands when they learned on their arrival that he had already been remanded for trial in advance of their own accusations. They quickly proceeded to draw up among themselves a long series of charges under fifty-seven separate headings, and placed these in La Gasca's hands.

Prior to their arrival, La Gasca had set his own investigations on foot and was principally concerned to obtain clear answers to the following five questions:

1. What was the state of affairs in Chile when Valdivia left it?

2. What was his object in coming to Peru, to help Pizarro or to serve the King?

3. Had he had any share in the death of Sancho de Hoz?

4. Had Sancho de Hoz any legitimate claim to the Chilean Governorship?

5. Would Valdivia's return to Chile be for the country's good?[4]

While proceeding with his own secret investigation, La Gasca passed on to Valdivia on October 30 a transcription of the fifty-seven charges preferred by his accusers, to all of which Valdivia made formal replies.

The charges referred to had been presented anonymously by their authors in order that their separate testimony as witnesses should be allowed as evidence in the court proceedings. Light is thrown upon La Gasca's estimate of and regard for Valdivia by the fact that he took pains to discover who the authors were and promptly ruled against their appearing as witnesses in a trial to which they were party.

It is clear that La Gasca's secret investigations had provided him with more than sufficient material with which to counteract the largely malicious accusations presented by Pedro de Villagra's companions. Furthermore, of the eleven men whom he finally admitted as witnesses, two only were definitely against Valdivia, and went far to destroy the value of their evidence by the absurd statement that Valdivia was lacking even in the elementary qualities of a soldier. Others, while attacking him on some points, defended him on the principal ones. It was still a majority, however, who showed themselves to be decided and even enthusiastic supporters of the accused.

On November 19, La Gasca pronounced the verdict unanimously reached by himself, the Archbishop of Lima, General Hinojosa, Marshall Alvarado, and Lorenzo de Aldana. Pedro de Valdivia was acquitted on all major counts and was confirmed in his governorship. There were, however, certain conditions attached to the verdict which cast reflections upon past conduct: he was instructed to put an immediate end to his relations with Inés de Suarez, and within a period of six months either to marry her or send her out of the country; he was to pay his debts; he was to see that all those who desired to leave Chile were permitted to do so; he was to pay special attention to the care of the landed estates and to the welfare of the Indian slaves who worked on them.

The following summary of the verdict sent by La Gasca to the Council of Indies on the November 26 of this year is not without interest:

"Considering," he says, "that Pedro de Valdivia conquered all that part of Chile which was at peace, and was sustaining it, and that he came to serve His Majesty in spite of Gonzalo Pizarro having sent with Baptista offers to win him over, with gifts of wine, preserves, cloth, and silks as appears in the said testimony;

"And considering how well and with what zeal he served His Majesty and labored in this enterprise and what he had spent on it, both on the ships and the men he took to Chile, so that between these things he had not only spent what he had but had sunk quite considerably into debt;

"And since if he did not return to his province he would never be able to pay either His Majesty or a number of private individuals what he owes them, and since he is the person who has most experience of affairs in that territory, and since our information is that he appears to unite in himself the other qualities required for subduing it and particularly that he is careful of the conservation and good treatment of the natives, which is one of the qualities most to be looked for in the *Conquistadores;*

"And considering how Pedro de Valdivia neither ordered the execution of Sancho de Hoz nor took any part in it, and that the said Sancho de Hoz had no commission whatsoever which might support his pretensions to the conquest of Chile, which was the point that weighed most with me in obliging Valdivia to return to Peru for examination, for it was put to me how unpardonable it would be to send Valdivia as Governor if it were true that he had killed Sancho de Hoz, reputed to have a title from His Majesty for the Governorship of that province, so that instead of punishing Valdivia for murdering the Governor I would be giving him the very same governorship;

"And considering also that the money he carried away on loan had merely been to send for help, and to come and to serve in this campaign and that on precisely this he spent it, and that the horses he was said to have taken had been for the war, and that the Spaniards he had killed had simply been executed in the course of justice as men who wished to stir up trouble and rebellion, disturbances which in these countries more than in others should be rigorously punished because of the frequency with which they are committed and the serious harm they cause. And as for keeping that woman, though it set a bad example it was hardly sufficient cause, from the point of view of how it was regarded among soldiers, for taking away his territory and his governorship;

"It therefore seemed to us all that he should be given freedom to take up the commission given to him in Cuzco as Governor and Captain General of the provinces of Chile."[5]

Valdivia lost no time in leaving Lima once his trial had been satisfactorily concluded. Undoubtedly, to him the most serious aspect of the delay it had caused was the fact that he had lost another summer season for the thing which was always uppermost in his mind, the opening up of the country south of Santiago. He made his way as rapidly as possible to Arequipa, where he arrived on December 24. Here he was taken seriously ill and for eight days was apparently in some danger of his life. After a short convalescence he pressed southwards, and on January 21, 1549, he set sail from Arica on the galleon *San Cristobal* with the two hundred new recruits whom he had additionally contrived to attract to his service.

Meanwhile Esteban de Sosa's force of eighty men, sent down, it will be recollected, ahead of Valdivia before his original departure from Lima and subsequent recall for trial, had caused considerable concern and even alarm in Santiago. News of the arrival in Copiapó of what was merely known to be a substantial force of Spaniards was conveyed to Andrés de Escobar, who had been stationed in La Serena by Francisco de Villagra precisely for the purpose of obtaining firsthand reports of this kind, and was quickly relayed to Santiago. The lack of news from Valdivia, and the sudden and unannounced arrival of a Spanish contingent from the north, might well portend a Pizarro triumph in Peru and the coming of a new Lieutenant Governor of the rebel faction, with incalculable consequences for the original Chilean colonists. Villagra considered the matter of sufficient consequence to leave Santiago himself and make a personal reconnaissance.

He set out at once with a small force for La Serena and thence proceeded cautiously northward, keeping himself advised by small advance parties of what lay ahead. The meeting with Sosa in Copiapó dispelled all his fears, and the combined forces made their way back to Santiago without further incident.

It had been Sosa's mission to gather supplies for Valdivia's other lieutenants bringing down parties of recruits. To guard these, Villagra left Juan Bohon in Copiapó with a force of twenty-nine men. Andrés de Escobar remained at his post in La Serena with a force of sixteen. Only three of these forty-seven Spaniards survived the next few weeks.

No sooner had Villagra returned to Santiago than the Indians fell on Bohon's force and destroyed it to a man. There being no survivors, we have no record of what carelessness or treachery can have been responsible for the wiping out of what was in those days a very respectable force in Indian warfare.

Andrés de Escobar soon began to notice the results in the behavior of the natives in the La Serena district. They had immediate news of the triumph of their neighbors in Copiapó and at once began to show signs of excitement and growing insolence. Escobar suspected that some disaster in Copiapó must be the cause, and as his principal function was to keep Villagra advised of events in the north, he decided himself to go to Santiago and warn him of what appeared to be serious trouble. He reached the capital on January 25 or 26, 1549.

Immediately after his departure, La Serena fell prey to the Indians, who, greatly emboldened by the news from Copiapó, called in the tribes from Huasco and Limarí and emulated the example of their countrymen farther north. The Spanish precautions again seem to have been most inadequate, for the natives were able to filter into the town during the night and to station themselves at the doors of all the houses without any alarm being given. Once all were at their posts they gave their bloodcurdling war cry (*chivateo*) and easily cut down each Spaniard individually as he rushed from his dwelling.

Two men only escaped. All the others, estimated at fourteen, were killed, and the buildings destroyed by fire. In addition to the Spaniards, a number of half-caste children and friendly Indians from Peru were also slaughtered. According to those Spaniards who afterwards saw the scene, a number of the victims died by impalement. The penalties for carelessness in this game with the Indians were serious.

The only two men who escaped finally reached Quintero in a state of collapse. Practically naked, hiding by day and walking by night, they had made their way down through a territory seething with the excitement of successful rebellion. The disastrous news they brought with them reached Santiago only five or six days after Escobar himself.

The *Cabildo* met on February 1 and commissioned Francisco de Villagra to proceed at once to the north to punish the rebels, leaving Francisco de Aguirre in command in Santiago. Villagra got together a force of seventy men, half cavalry and half infantry, an unspecified number of the latter being arquebusiers who were sent up by sea. Villagra led the main force overland.

The sea expedition arrived first and disembarked. Making use of such walls as were found standing, they dug themselves in with the object of making sorties against the enemy as opportunity offered. They were, however, soon put on the defensive by the now thoroughly truculent natives, and when after five days' hard fighting they had lost two of their number, they resolved to return to their ship and await Villagra's arrival. He joined them the next day, about fifteen days after leaving Santiago.

At almost the same moment, the various parties recruited in Peru by Valdivia's lieutenants reached Copiapó. Juan Jufré and Cristobal de la Cueva had managed to gather only a small force between them. Jufré, on making contact with Valdivia's original party, which had been left to continue its journey south in charge of Ulloa, arrested the latter and took supreme command. Not long afterward, Pedro de Villagra joined this group and united them all under himself. As Valdivia had feared, his own return to Peru and the consequent jealous squabbling among his lieutenants had caused considerable dispersion of his followers, and Pedro de Villagra found himself at the head of a force totaling not more than ninety to a hundred men. He was hard pressed by the Indians in his passage across the desert and in the Copiapó valley, but was finally able to negotiate an unexpected truce with them, unaware that Francisco de Villagra was at that moment advancing northward on his punitive expedition and that the natives were afraid of being caught between two fires. His further passage south was without incident.

The disasters at Copiapó and La Serena had considerably quickened the apprehensions of the inhabitants of Santiago regarding their own safety. It was a natural supposition that the successes of the natives in the north would have a disagreeably heartening effect on those in Aconcagua and Cachapoal, and Francisco de Villagra's departure with seventy men provided an excellent opportunity for an attack if they cared to take it. Precautions of every kind were redoubled, and Francisco de Aguirre found it necessary to lead out a small force to quell a rising near the Cachapoal. It was, however, at Marga-Marga that the alarm was most keenly felt, and the miners there made a written demand in no uncertain terms for an extra guard of six men to be sent to them by the *Cabildo*. When the *Cabildo* agreed to the provision of only four men, the miners struck and abandoned the workings. It was only the arrival in April of Pedro de Valdivia himself, with his two hundred additional recruits, that restored some sense of tranquillity to the anxious community.

In his voyage down the coast Valdivia had put in at La Serena, which he found deserted and in ruins. Learning of Francisco de Villagra's presence in the vicinity, news which he probably extracted from some local Indian by those means which "were understood," he and Jeronimo de Alderete left letters for Villagra to discover on his return. Alderete's letter merely contained news of the confirmation of Valdivia's appointment as Governor. Valdivia's own communication commanded Villagra to put an end to his punitive expeditions and to remain in La Serena until he received further instructions.

Villagra's men, on returning to La Serena, saw written in large letters on an oven[6] the message "Dig where the old cross used to be." On doing so they found Valdivia's letter, which was soon in Villagra's hands.

Villagra had small wish to stay in the north indefinitely, and he was naturally most anxious both to give Valdivia an account of all that had happened in his absence and himself to learn what had taken place in Peru. To proceed south, however, meant taking a substantial proportion of his forces with him and thus dangerously weakening the garrison in defiance of the Governor's instructions. He was relieved of this dilemma by the timely arrival of a vessel from Peru carrying Vicencio de Monte and his family to Valparaiso. This was an opportunity not to be missed, and Villagra accompanied de Monte on the remainder of his voyage, after transferring his command to Diego de Maldonado. He reached Valparaiso in April, not long after Valdivia himself.

If any proof of Villagra's loyalty and devotion were needed, at all events in Valdivia's mind, it is provided by the accounts of the meeting between these old friends. Valdivia immediately confirmed him in his position of Lieutenant Governor and, two days after himself taking his office as Governor, designated him his Lieutenant General. In this latter ceremony, after the customary praises for a man who "is held as a gentleman and hidalgo," he said, "Of all that with which I charged you in His Majesty's name, you have rendered me the just and excellent account which gentlemen of your profession and caliber are accustomed to give."[7] The tribute is specific and unstinted, and it is difficult to suppose that a man of Valdivia's experience could have been blind to the kind of duplicity supposed by Gongora Marmolejo, had it really existed.

The *Cabildo* found plenty to engage its attention on the Governor's return. On May 2, Jeronimo de Alderete presented his credentials, granted originally by Blasco Nuñez, the Peruvian Viceroy, and confirmed by La Gasca, as Royal Treasurer. On the 29th, Esteban de Sosa and Vicencio de Monte presented their nominations as Controller and Overseer respectively, both being appointments made by La Gasca. Finally, there was Pedro de Valdivia himself to be formally received as Governor. The occasion was to provide a trial of strength between the founder of the colony and the body which, although originally his own creation, had inevitably grown considerably in the sense of its own power and prestige in his absence.

The *Cabildo* opened the gambit by courteously demanding that, before being received as Governor, Valdivia should take the usual oath to keep the laws and to uphold the privileges and maintain the rights and rewards which had been won by the colonists. Valdivia considered that the oath which he had originally sworn on taking office as Governor-Elect was sufficient. Not wishing, however, openly to oppose the *Cabildo*, he gave a qualified assent by stating that Jeronimo de Alderete, with his full power, and aided by his secretary, Juan de Cardenas, would take the oath on his behalf. The *Cabildo* in their turn accepted the proposal unanimously, and once Alderete had duly taken the oath, they proceeded publicly to proclaim Valdivia as Governor in the King's name without further ado.

The matter seemed to have been arranged to the satisfaction of both sides. But in fact all was not yet over. On the following day, the Governor, now appointed by the King and no longer elected by his fellows, made his ceremonial entry into Santiago. He was received with the pomp and solemnity which befitted the occasion. All accompanied the Governor to his house, and once arrived there the *Cabildo* made their next preconcerted move. In the presence of the Notary Public, Luis de Cartagena, they respectfully requested the Governor to repeat in person the oath made in his name by Alderete the previous day, since, they alleged, this would not only be in accordance with established custom, but would shed even greater luster on the high office which he had just assumed.

Among those implicated in the request Valdivia observed

Francisco de Villagra

his staunch friends Francisco de Villagra, Juan Fernandez de Alderete, Francisco de Aguirre, Rodrigo de Quiroga, Esteban de Sosa, and many others, nor did he hear anywhere any voice raised against the proposal. There was nothing for it but to submit, though he protested that in view of his royal appointment and his public reception as Governor after the oath had been taken by his delegate, he had thought that what was done was enough. And the Minutes record, "Now again he promises, and he promised, and swore as a gentleman and hidalgo, and clasped his hands one against the other, and he swore in due and lawful manner to do and to keep all that Jeronimo de Alderete had bound him in his name to do and to keep." The *Cabildo* waited quietly and patiently for this ceremony to be over, but they were still not to be put off. Valdivia had sworn as "a gentleman and hidalgo" with clasped hands, amounting only to a solemn promise. This was not the oath proper to a governor nor the one they had requested.

Valdivia accepted this diplomatic defeat gracefully. "And he swore," say the Minutes, "by God and by St. Mary and by a Cross on which he laid his right hand . . . and in confirmation of the said oath, he said 'Yes, I swear and amen.'"

BOLIVIA

• Cotagaita

• Sococha

• Jujuy

• El Barco
• Tucumán

Santiago
del Estero

THE ANDES

A R G E N T I N A

La Serena •

R. LIMARI
R. CHOAPA

La Ligua • Quillota
Concón • • Quillota   Aconcagua
Valparaíso • • Quilicura   Valley
Marga-Marga • • Mendoza
Santa Maria   Santiago
R. RAPEL R. CACHAPOAL

Penco •
Pte.   • Concepción
LAVAPIE
Arauco • R. LAJA
Tucapel • Quilaco
• Purén Angol (Los Confines)
Imperial • R. CAUTEN
(Nueva Imperial)
Villarrica • • Pucón
Valdivia •   Valley
R. CALLE-CALLE
Corral •
Rio Negro •
San Pedro •

Canal de Chacao

CENTRAL

CHILE

Land over 5000 ft. elevation

GULF OF
RELONCAVI

Miles

0   200

M.E.S.

11

The Opening
Up
of the South

To further the task of extending his domains southward, the design which was always uppermost in Valdivia's mind, two main problems had to be solved. Firstly, further recruits would become increasingly necessary to populate the new territories and to hold down their native inhabitants, and secondly, communications with Peru in his rear must be firmly consolidated and cease to be exposed to the kind of disaster which had recently overtaken Bohon in Copiapó and the garrison in La Serena.

To meet the first of these requirements, Valdivia chose Francisco de Villagra as his envoy to Peru for the recruitment of reinforcements, an appointment which was received with general satisfaction by the colony.

By those who have believed in Villagra's duplicity, this move has been interpreted as a maneuver on the part of Valdivia to rid himself of a man he did not trust. A little thought, however, seems to throw the balance of probability in precisely the reverse direction. The consequences of sending unreliable ambassadors to Peru had surely been too amply demonstrated by Antonio de Ulloa to make Valdivia ambitious to repeat so costly an experiment. Furthermore, it was now more than ever important to him that a good account of his reception in Chile should reach La Gasca in order finally to dispel whatever lingering doubts might have remained in the astute ecclesiastic's mind regarding Valdivia's suitability for his post. An entirely satisfactory account could only come with certainty from a trusted friend. Villagra's appointment would on these grounds appear, so far from indicating mistrust, to afford striking additional proof of Valdivia's absolute confidence in him.

Villagra left Valparaiso by sea on July 9th and reached Lima on August 20th, having among his company his relative Gabriel de Villagra, who had recently come down from Peru with Valdivia.

For his second objective of bringing the north under firm control, Valdivia chose Francisco de Aguirre, naming him Lieutenant Governor of the district between Atacama and the river Choapa. Aguirre was to be responsible directly to Valdivia in his new post and was made independent of any subjection to Valdivia's Lieutenant General and second-in-command, Francisco de Villagra. His principal objectives were to refound the town of La Serena and to keep open the lines of communication with Peru. He was also granted powers for the distribution of landed estates and Indian labor.

Aguirre left Santiago in mid-July with five Spaniards and three hundred Indian auxiliaries, but would also have under his command a force of some fifty other Spaniards whom Francisco de Villagra had left in the north under the command of Diego de Maldonado.

Maldonado had already made some progress with the rebuilding of La Serena, and Pedro de Villagra, before finally completing his journey through to Santiago, had managed to pacify the district from Copiapó south after making a truce, as will be recalled, with the natives of Copiapó itself. Pedro de Villagra appears, indeed, to have obtained some singularly successful results in this part of the country by moderate and peaceful means, his crowning achievement being to gain the friendship of Michimalongo and to bring him down with him to Santiago. The converted chieftain remained a firm ally of the Spaniards from that time onward and served them well with a substantial force of Indian auxiliaries.

Pedro de Villagra's unquestionably solid and constructive work was belittled by Aguirre, who wished it to be thought that he alone was responsible for bringing the north into final subservience. His methods were very different from those of the man it was his interest to belittle.

After refounding La Serena on August 26, 1549, Aguirre lost no time in giving the natives a taste of his quality. Setting out for Copiapó, he found the Indians in peaceful mood, either from respect for the quality of his force or because they were genuinely tired of the unceasing and unequal struggle. Their friendly gestures availed them nothing. Aguirre rounded up all the principal chieftains and burnt them at the stake, and he appears to have followed up this performance with other repressive measures of the most ruthless kind.

Aguirre boasts of having settled the northern province in so conclusive a manner that the natives never seriously bothered the Spaniards again. So far as his statement goes, he is factually correct. It is, however, fair comment to say that he gained his objective not so much by leaving peaceful Indians in his wake as by leaving practically no Indians in his wake at all.

Valdivia's decision to make the northern province inde-pendent under its own Lieutenant Governor did not pass without opposition from the *Cabildo* in Santiago, whose boundaries had hitherto extended from the river Itata in the south to Copiapó in the north. The *Cabildo* reacted to Valdivia's move by requesting that these boundaries should be confirmed and that Santiago should be declared the capital of the colony.

Valdivia acceded to the second part of the request and declared Santiago the seat of the federal government, if we may so describe it. For municipal purposes, however, the new northern boundary of its jurisdiction was fixed on the river Choapa. Two limitations were, nevertheless, imposed on Aguirre's province: it was to provide troops for service against the natives when called upon to do so by the *Cabildo* in Santiago, and insofar as the administration of law was concerned, it was to be subject to the Chief Justice, whose seat also was in the capital.

Valdivia was now ready to devote himself to the preparations for his southern campaign. Misfortune, however, continued to follow him. While reviewing his men on September 8, his horse fell and crushed one of his feet. The accident confined him to a couch for three months, and complications at one time appear to have put his life in danger. Even in this condition, however, he continued to concern himself feverishly with the preparations for the expedition, as well as for the proper care of Santiago in his absence.

Certainly those who were to remain behind were not without anxiety. The expedition would greatly reduce the size of the garrison and would in addition take with it a very large number of natives, some to carry the baggage and others to act as fighting auxiliaries. A rumor began to circulate that some of the expeditionaries were even preparing chains to ensure that the natives had no chance to abandon the force on the march and return to the capital. These apprehensions on the part of the citizens of Santiago became so acute that it was found necessary to apprise Valdivia of their existence in the form of a petition.

His answers were spirited and characteristic. Even after the expedition's departure, there would remain more men in Santiago than the original 150 soldiers with whom he had founded it. Let those that stayed, therefore, fight as he had had to fight. As regards the natives, he promised that these would be allowed to return as soon as Santiago's southern boundary, the Itata, was reached. Furthermore, as his petitioners should already know, he never had nor ever would permit the use of chains. Finally, he gave the *Cabildo* power to appoint a military commander of their own choosing in his absence, and to depose him and appoint another as frequently as they thought fit.

By the beginning of December, Valdivia was able to leave his couch. Time was drawing on, and he was becoming desperately impatient to be started. As against the protests of his friends, who tried to restrain him on the elementary grounds of his being still unable to put foot to stirrup, the thought of losing another year was quite intolerable to him. And so in early January the expedition set forth, Valdivia carried by hand in a litter.

The three hundred years' war between Spaniard and Araucanian was now to start in earnest. On more than one occasion, it was to place the colony on the borders of ruin and extinction. It would oblige the proud monarch of Castille, as Crescente Errazuriz puts it, to recognize a number of half-naked savages as belligerents defending their country with

171

astonishing vigor and intelligence. The struggle is in fact quite unique in history if we judge it, not by the size of the forces engaged, but by the unsurpassed heroism and tenacity with which it was fought by ten successive generations.

The Spaniards' superiority in arms, especially at the beginning, was overwhelming. Though they had no cannon before Valdivia's death and though their only firearms at this period were arquebuses, which, clumsy as they were and difficult to manage, must still have had considerable moral value in the opening stages, their swords and lances were of deadly effect, above all in the hands of men mounted on horseback and covered with armor which made them practically impervious to the missiles of their antagonists.

To all this the Araucanian could at first oppose only his arrows, his pikes and spears, and his clumsy clubs and axes, formidable as the latter were at close quarters in the hands of a powerful and determined savage. But as the numbers of the Spaniards increased, so did the Indians' tactics and weapons improve as they gradually gained possession and taught themselves to use the arms of the invaders. While from Valdivia's correspondence we can deduce that he sensed something of the vast difference between the Araucanian and his native contemporaries, it was undoubtedly not until after his death that the Spaniards began to comprehend fully the unique fighting qualities of this obscure and remarkable race.

Valdivia's force consisted of two hundred horse and foot and an unspecified but undoubtedly considerable number of *Picunche* auxiliaries commanded by Michimalongo. Pedro de Villagra, growing rapidly in Valdivia's esteem, was chief of staff and the expedition itself was divided into four companies commanded by Valdivia, Villagra, Alderete, and Diego de Oro respectively.

After an uneventful march of twenty days' duration, the expedition reached the river Itata. Here Valdivia, now able to ride again, sent back all the native porters as he had promised, but retained his *Picunche* auxiliaries under Michimalongo.

Beyond the Itata a few minor skirmishes took place, but it was not until the river Laja was reached that any serious resistance was encountered. At this point, Pedro de Villagra had some difficulty in beating off a determined attack by an enemy force estimated by Valdivia at two thousand strong.

The river Bío-Bío was reached on January 24, and here again a number of skirmishes took place. Finding a suitable ford up river, Valdivia decided to cross over to disperse the large numbers of natives threatening him from the further bank, a task which was successfully accomplished by a charge of fifty horse. He then retraced his steps and made his way toward the coast and the valley of Andalien, which he had already prospected in his expedition of four years before.

At about 10 o'clock on the second night after his arrival there, the Araucanians attacked him in force, numbering according to undoubtedly exaggerated contemporary accounts between fifteen and twenty thousand warriors. Valdivia had secured his rear on the side of a lake and was thus able to fight on a single front. This may have saved what at one moment was an ugly situation. The Indians appear to have concentrated their attentions upon the horses with such success that the beasts finally refused to face them.

"It was a beautiful encounter and battle by night with the sound of the Indians giving their orders and commands with a horn (by this they understood what to do) and their Captains encouraging them with the many things they said. . . . On the part of the Christians it was a brave thing to hear the thunder of the horses, the great sound of the trumpets, and the voice of Valdivia driving them on to break the Indians . . . And when the horses, well protected as they were, reached the Indians, the latter aimed such stunning blows at their heads with their clubs that they forced them backward and the horses could no longer be induced to face them; in addition the Indians rained such showers of arrows that nearly all the Spaniards were wounded and were sorely pressed and losing ground . . . Seeing that things were going against him . . . Pedro de Valdivia ordered some of his Captains to dismount . . . many others followed suit. Valdivia at the same time attacked with thirty soldiers in the rear and pressed the natives so closely that, seeing themselves surrounded . . . and the heaps of their dead around them, they lost heart, turned their backs, and fled."[1]

Only one Spaniard lost his life in the affray (he was killed by the careless shot of one of the Spanish arquebusiers), but sixty were wounded in various degrees. Sixty horses had also been severely handled. As usual, the losses of the auxiliaries are not recorded.

This battle was never forgotten by those who took part in it, and there seems little doubt that there was a moment in the midst of it when a disastrous defeat was more than a mere possibility. Though the natives were still not subjected to the discipline and planned tactics which were to give them such resounding successes three to four years hence, their sheer fighting energy and magnificent courage had brought them to the verge of defeating a really powerful force of well-equipped Spaniards. It was to this battle that Valdivia referred when he told the King, "I have warred with men of many nations, but never have I seen such fighting tenacity as is displayed by these Indians." It was of this battle that he was to be reminded by his servant Agustinillo when approaching Tucapel, the scene of the Araucanians' first tactically planned attack and of his own death. The tragedy is that while his own words proved that the different quality of the Araucanians had become apparent to him, he could never become entirely convinced that they could really be anything but the undisciplined savages he was so accustomed to see broken before his armor and ridden down by his cavalry. His final awakening was to come too late to save him.

The search for the site of the new city was continued, and the decision was finally reached to use that which Valdivia had provisionally selected four years before, namely Penco, described by Valdivia to the King as being "in a port and bay of which there is not the like in all the Indies, and a large river on one side running into the sea and the best fishing in the world . . . and on the other side a small stream that runs all year round, of clear sparkling water."

The obvious aggressiveness of the surrounding population made fortifications desirable; once the site of the city had been definitely fixed, Valdivia pitched his camp there, and on the following day, February 24, 1550, himself set the personal example of laboring on the construction of the defenses. In eight days a substantial stone and adobe wall had been completed of such size and strength that Valdivia was able to boast that he could defend it against the best soldiers in the world. He was not alive four years later to see it abandoned to the mercies of a victorious Araucanian army.

The interval of from fifteen to twenty days which the

Spaniards had spent in choosing their site and fortifying it had not been wasted by their Indian foes, who had organized a tremendous gathering of warriors from all directions. On March 12 they took the field with a force estimated by Valdivia at eighty thousand strong. The most careful calculations which it has been possible to make in regard to the total Araucanian population show that it is highly improbable that they could ever have put into the field at one time a total of more than fifty thousand men; fifteen thousand, or at the most twenty thousand, would seem to be the likely sort of maximum on this occasion. It must be admitted, however, that there is no real basis for fixing any definite figure, contemporary accounts agreeing merely on the facts that the Indians were an "infinite mass" and divided into four separate squadrons. So confident were they that they came with large numbers of ladders to scale the fortifications, and halters to lead away their prisoners.

Valdivia's description of what he saw before the battle is worth recording and greatly helps us to picture the kind of scene the Spaniards faced in their innumerable fights with the Araucanians.

"On they came with the utmost boldness, four divisions of the finest and most splendid Indians that have been seen in these parts, excellently protected with the undressed skins of llamas and sheep and seals, of a variety of colors, a most stirring sight to behold with the tall plumes on their helmets, which were fashioned from those same skins, like the great hats of priests, and there is no battle-axe, however sharp, which can harm those that wear them."

The Governor's thought was to await the attack behind his fortifications, and he gave instructions to Pedro de Villagra, who was outside with a few soldiers, to come in. Villagra obeyed, but with no intention of staying there. He argued that to stay where they were was equivalent to asking to be swamped by vastly superior numbers and to be deprived of their greatest daylight advantage, the use of their horses. Valdivia admitted the force of the reasoning and ordered Villagra with his few men, and Alderete with fifty more, to sally forth against the enemy. The infantry also marched out and advanced behind the horse.

Events completely justified Villagra, not infrequently found to be a better general than Valdivia himself. The first vigorous charge of the cavalry produced chaos in the leading Indian squadron, which broke up in rout and spread panic among the rest. What followed was not a battle but simply pursuit and butchery, and the field was strewn with bodies of two thousand Indian dead. The Spaniards also took four hundred prisoners.

The treatment accorded to these prisoners is perhaps the greatest single blot on Valdivia's record, not only morally but from the point of view of policy. The nose and the right hand of each of these wretches was cut off, and they were then let go to spread terror among their fellows.[2] All that they could in fact have spread was the grimmest of determinations to die fighting rather than ever submit. If anything was still required to harden an implacable resistance, this surely was a sovereign method of providing it.

If we dwell imaginatively for a moment on the actual procedure of executing this hideous punishment, in cold blood, on four hundred separate individuals one after the other, we can hardly cerdit what is, nevertheless, a well authenticated fact. The best that can be said is that the Spaniards at least had the excuse, however mistaken they may have been in their judgment of policy, that if they were to carry their project through, they had somehow to dominate numbers amounting to many hundred times their own, and these of men whom they regarded as little better than animals and dangerous fighting animals into the bargain.

The complete collapse of the Araucanians on this occasion caused the Spaniards some surprise, and as a result the story of a miracle gained a good deal of credence. The story is in two separate parts. Firstly, it was believed that the Virgin Mary appeared to the Indians three days before the battle, dressed in white and most beautiful in appearance, and said to them, "Serve the Christians and go not against them, for they are passing brave and will kill you all." And secondly, just as the Spaniards charged, the Apostle James, in the guise of an old man on a white horse, came down among the Indian companies saying, "Flee, all of you, for these Christians will slay you." The historian and ecclesiastic Crescente Errazuriz, Primate of all Chile, had a special interest in sifting the evidence for this legend, and sums up roundly against it.

That for which there is incontrovertible evidence is the fact of a meteorite of extraordinary brilliance having fallen into the river as the Indians were crossing on March 9th. Indians and Spaniards alike were agreed on this. Without question, such an occurrence at so critical a moment would have been taken as an omen by the superstitious natives, and it may well explain why after crossing the river on the 9th they delayed the deployment of their forces for attack until the 12th. We may suppose them to have occupied the interval in having the phenomenon interpreted by the witch doctors and to have reached only a half hearted decision to attack in a spirit of considerable doubt and misgiving. Possibly some adverse sign of a purely casual nature, but of a kind of which the *Voigenvoes* had warned them to beware, manifested itself when the Spaniards came out against them and confirmed their worst estimate of the real meaning of the meteorite. All this can be no more than the merest supposition, but the headlong flight of so large a force of fighting Araucanians at the very first onset of the Spaniards, so entirely inconsistent with their behavior on countless other occasions, does demand an explanation which all the known facts fail to supply.

Eight days after the attack on Penco, Juan Bautista de Pastene arrived with two ships and a reinforcement of fifty men. Accompanying him was the ecclesiastic Rodrigo Gonzalez de Marmolejo, whom Valdivia had sent back to Santiago earlier to coax further reinforcements out of the *Cabildo* and to obtain fresh supplies. Valdivia's estimate of the persuasive powers of his friend proved well-founded. With the additonal forces now at his disposal, Valdivia proceeded to organize two expeditions, one by sea under Pastene and the other by land under Alderete, who was given sixty horsemen. Both brought back excellent tidings.

Pastene reached the island called Talca by the Indians, the Santa María of today, and described it in glowing terms. The natives had received him in the friendliest manner and had supplied him with abundant provisions.

Alderete, commissioned to explore Arauco, had an equally easy time, due no doubt in great measure to the resounding reverse just suffered by the natives at Penco. A few Indians watched the novel spectacle of the Spaniards crossing the Bío-Bío by the expedient of holding on to the tails of their horses in the water, but they offered no resistance and dispersed when the Spaniards gained the southern bank. The expedition advanced as far as the river Cautín and returned by way of the present site of the town of Angol.

Alderete brought back promises of peace and obedience from such natives as he had encountered, offers which must have excited the liveliest hopes of wealth and contentment in the minds of the Spaniards who had now some knowledge of the magnificent country which lay all around them and of the abundance of its potential labor force. Centuries were, nevertheless, to pass before the hopes in regard to this particular area were to be fully realized. Alderete also brought back a number of Indian chieftains as prisoners, and ingenuously attributed to this simple fact the apparent pacification of a territory which was for many generations to swallow up countless Spanish lives.

Winter was now approaching, but Valdivia's impatience could brook no interruption to his progress. He commissioned Pedro de Villagra, undoubtedly the ablest soldier serving under him, to continue to explore the surrounding country in all directions and to obtain assurances of peace from the natives. The commission was no sinecure. Though the disaster at Penco had chastened the Indians and assured their quiescence for the time being, the heavy rains and swollen rivers made traveling not merely arduous but dangerous. Villagra doggedly carried out his instructions right through the winter from April to November, 1550, taking out different parties by turns but himself constantly on the move.

In August, as spring was approaching, Pastene was again ordered south, this time for the specific purpose of bringing back some of the friendly Indians from the island of Santa Maria to be used as ambassadors to the more refractory elements in the surrounding population. They were to convey to their neighbors on the mainland a message of the great need for giving the required assurances of peace on the grounds that, if they were not given, war and death would swiftly follow. A strange method, comments Errazuriz, of seeking friendship.

Pastene sailed with two vessels and soon had a suitable number of natives from Santa Maria in his power. After passing the point of Lavapié, he came in sight of the bay which was afterwards named Carnero. Here the appearance of a substantial population engaged his attention, and he decided to put ashore a party of twenty men to obtain supplies and to make contact with the chieftains. The Indians, for their part, made unseen preparations to attack the invaders and called upon their neighbors to rally to their assistance. They then lay in ambush in the neighboring woods.

The Spaniards duly came ashore and, finding none to say them nay, proceeded not merely to help themselves to whatever supplies seemed likely to be of use to them, but to violate the Indian women who had been left unprotected by their menfolk. With additional fury lent by the sight of these excesses, the Indian warriors broke ambush and fell upon their invaders.

The fight was both keen and costly. Before reaching their boat and making good their withdrawal, the Spaniards had lost no less than a third of their number. This incident is mentioned both by Gongora Marmolejo and Mariño de Lobera, but nowhere by Pedro de Valdivia in his correspondence to Charles V. Since it occurred only a few weeks before the date of his most famous dispatches, forwarded on October 15 of this same year, in which he describes in detail the events of many years, the omission can hardly be attributed to forgetfulness. We must conclude that he recognized it as being hardly the kind of incident which would have embellished the picture he wished his Monarch to have before him.

Another specific part of Pastene's mission was to obtain supplies from the island of La Mocha. Very different was his reception here. The natives were generous in the extreme and pressed food upon these strange beings whose like they had never seen before. Mariño de Lobera expresses indignation at the Spaniards' method of retribution for such kindness. After stowing their supplies safely aboard, the Spaniards fell upon their hosts and dragged as many as they could, men and women alike, to their ships and carried them away as captives. The reasons for this action are not clear, but they were presumably based on Valdivia's desire to send friendly and submissive natives as ambassadors of peace among the more recalcitrant. If this is the true solution, the psychological aspect of the approach does not cease to be puzzling.

Pastene returned from his mission in the middle of September. He was sent out on a third voyage shortly afterward for the two objects of obtaining further supplies and continuing to extract assurances of peace from any natives found on the coast.

On October 5, 1550, the new city at Penco was formally declared founded. It was to be known as *Concepción del Nuevo Extremo,* and its boundaries were the river Maule in the north and the Lavapié in the south, the whole of this territory being considered as now firmly in the invaders' hands.[3] Landed estates were distributed in a number which at this time remained unspecified, but was definitely fixed at forty in April of the following year.

Valdivia had dedicated some part of the winter to the compiling of two long descriptive letters, one to King Charles V, and the other to what are described as his representatives at the Court. The second of these documents was really directed to the Council of Indies to act as a permanent record of his services to the Crown generally and of his achievements in Chile in particular. The two documents are very similar in subject matter and even in wording, though each contains certain incidents missing in the other and they are to that extent mutually complementary. They form one of the principal sources of·information on the events in the young colony which we have so far recorded.

The representatives selected by Valdivia to bear these messages to Spain were Rodrigo Gonzalez de Marmolejo, the priest so devoted to Valdivia's service, and Alonso de Aguilera. The latter had only recently arrived in Chile and had family ties with the Governor.

Gonzalez did not in fact make the journey. When the news of his impending departure became public, both the *Cabildo* and people of Santiago threw themselves at the old man's feet—the words are Valdivia's—and begged him not to abandon them. The good cleric was not proof against this demonstration, and abandoning further thoughts of Spain, he made up his mind to spend such years as were left to him in his new country.

In his letter to Charles V, Valdivia begs the King, instead of looking for a bishop for Chile among his "cloisters and convents," to choose one who had the advantage of being already in the place where he was required and to elevate Gonzalez to the post. Gonzalez, for his part, in spite of his advanced age, continued to serve in the forefront of the expedition and was present at the founding of both Imperial and Valdivia. When we add to this the fact that he had on his own initiative introduced horse-breeding into the colony, and had thereby both done it a great practical service and made himself a modest fortune, it will be seen that here was a man of many parts. The generous uses to which he put his money and his blameless life had won him universal respect. It is difficult to see how a better choice for the ecclesiastical head of the colony could have been made.

The rewards requested of his monarch by Valdivia are of considerable interest, above all because of the necessary relationship they bear to the sort of recompense which a man of Valdivia's achievements could expect to receive at this period. He asks for the Governorship of Chile for his own life and for those of two heirs, either of his body or whomsoever else he shall designate; the right to appoint incumbents to the offices of Surveyor-General, Notaries Public, *Cabildo,* and three Councilors in each municipality; authority to build three or four fortresses, endowed with lands and native labor, of which he and his heirs shall be lieutenants with a yearly stipend of a *cuento de maravedis*[4] for each fortress; the benefit of one-eighth of all territory subjugated—with the right to select the eighth—in perpetuity for himself and his descendants; and finally a salary of 10,000 *Castellanos* a year, the remission of a debt of 118,000 *Castellanos,* and a bonus of a further 100,000 *Castellanos.* Valdivia's modest description of himself as a man of arms, not of letters or business judgment, is again brought sharply to mind.

Before leaving Concepción for the 1550-51 campaigning season, Valdivia took several steps which he considered of importance. The soldiery had set great hopes on the gold-mining possibilities of the south. "Nowhere do you dig but you find gold"[5] was their greatly exaggerated description of this potential wealth. If ideas of this sort remained unchecked, the possibilites of disaster were only too evident. The Indians were little disposed to regular work of any kind, and above all they hated the hard labor involved in mining. If anything were required to stiffen their will to resist, individual fortune hunting on the grand scale would be the surest way to provide it. It was equally clear that the soldiers found the glamor of gold prospecting far more attractive than the humdrum of building dwellings and fortifications. On both counts Valdivia was obviously wise to aim at security first and to leave more speculative projects, however enticing, to a more appropriate period. He accordingly prohibited all mining activity until such time as he saw in Concepción a satisfactory number of buildings of bricks and tiles.

To forestall the natural alarm which the founding of the city, and especially the distribution of estates and labor, would clearly cause among the natives, Valdivia called the principal chieftains of the area to a meeting on October 7, two days after the founding ceremony. By means of interpreters, he told them that the King of Spain had sent him, not to obtain possession of their dwellings, land, or livestock, but to govern them in justice, instruct them in religion, and procure their conversion to the Catholic faith. The Indians listened to what, not entirely without reason, they regarded as sheer hypocrisy and made every promise the Governor could require. It is perhaps only fair to say that neither side really meant what they said.

The Indians' whole attitude at this period, stemming largely from their severe defeat at Penco (now renamed Concepción) and concealing as it did their true fighting nature and their amazing capacity for hitting back, was perhaps the one thing required to complete Valdivia's destruction. He had never yet encountered any natives who could long withstand the Spaniards' superiority in arms and intelligence, and he could hardly be blamed if what he had recently seen of the Araucanians merely went to confirm everything that the whole of his previous experience had taught him. His impatient aim was still to advance to the Straits of Magellan, and the next logical step was to set up another milestone on the road by founding a new city south of the Bío-Bío, inevitably bringing with it a further dispersal and thinning out of the Spanish forces.

A clearer picture of his danger, as can not infrequently occur, was visible to those who were not so directly involved and were in fact far distant from the scene of action. The authorites in Spain, in spite of their being no more aware than Valdivia of the real qualities of the Araucanian warrior, were presumably receiving information from other sources than simply the rather infrequent letters of Valdivia himself. If we remember the apprehensions of the citizens in Santiago when Valdivia was preparing to go south at the end of 1549, it is possible to suppose that at least some part of these fears would be communicated by individuals, as opportunity offered, to friends and relations in the mother country, and thence find

Be this as it may, in an official communication from the Court to the Royal Audience at Lima, dated November 25, 1551, or approximately a year later than the point we have so far reached, there is mention of the excellent news from Chile and a recommendation to send to the promising territory whatever reinforcements could be spared from Peru. But the communication goes further than mere recommendation when it categorically orders that all effort should now be concentrated on consolidating what was already held, and that further conquest should be halted until this primary objective had been satisfactorily and securely achieved. The communication adds that instructions to this effect are to be sent to Chile immediately. We can suppose this document to have reached Peru in the first half of 1552, and the rescript should have been in Valdivia's hands at latest by the end of the same year. Whether it in fact arrived after the catastrophe of December, 1553, or was received by him before his death and simply disregarded in his blind desire to press southward, there is no evidence now to show. What we do know is that the foresight shown by the Spanish authorities had no practical influence on the march of events.

Free from all apprehensions of the danger which those in Spain were already sensing, in the middle of February, 1551, Valdivia set out to forge the further link in his proposed chain of settlements to the south. Before leaving Concepción, he built a further adobe wall round the infant town about ten feet in height and four feet thick, calculating this to be sufficient defense for the garrision of fifty men, including twenty horse, whom he left there. At the head of seventy Spaniards, he soon afterwards joined Alderete and Pedro de Villagra south of the Bío-Bío and entered the territory of Arauco in command of a combined force of 170 men, of whom 120 were cavalry.

In spite of messages sent through interpreters to the surrounding tribes, disclosing to them the benefits which would allegedly accrue to them from voluntarily giving their obedience to the Spanish King, an obedience which Valdivia added that he would in any other event extract from them by force, the natives showed no signs of conviction and attacked him at frequent intervals. His well-armed force, however, had no difficulty in beating off these sporadic thrusts, which were still entirely lacking in the disciplined organization and cohesion which must by now have begun to germinate among the main Araucanian forces lying concealed and as yet dispersed among the woodland fastnesses of the country.

After a thorough investigation into the possibilities for a suitable site, the decision was taken to found the new town at the junction of the river Cautín with one of its tributaries, the Las Damas. The decision once taken, the next ten or twelve days were spent in constructing a fort, greatly superior in Valdivia's opinion to that of Penco.

On April 4th, Valdivia returned to Concepción with twenty horse, leaving Pedro de Villagra to carry on the work of building up the new settlement. Apart from desiring to spend the winter in Concepción, Valdivia was anxious about the arrival of two ships which he was expecting from Peru, and he wished also to make definite the distribution of the estates granted in the Concepción area, this having been only provisionally settled at the time of the formal foundation ceremony. It may be mentioned that his difficulties were considerably lighter here than they had been in Santiago. The vast lands of the south, abundantly watered and rich in produce and native population, were now a matter no longer of conjecture, but of proven fact. Those who received no reward in Concepción could confidently expect to receive an even richer prize farther south. That it would also be considerably safer farther south was an advantage which was as yet not perceptible.

The vessels from Peru duly arrived in June and in addition to abundant supplies brought a reinforcement of a further one hundred men. The Governor at once lifted his eyes to yet more distant horizons with such a substantial additional force at his disposal.

It was probably at this time that Valdivia received from Peru a transcription of a letter from the King to La Gasca, in which the monarch recognizes Valdivia's services to the Crown and commands that they be kept in mind. While it contained no mention of any immediate reward, it was nevertheless satisfactory confirmation of recognition in high places and constituted a solid source of hope and encouragement.

Two days after the arrival of these vessels, further excellent news was received. Diego de Maldonado had crossed the Andes with eight men to inform Valdivia that Francisco de Villagra was back again in Cuyo, east of the Andes and on a level with Santiago, with a force of two hundred well-equipped recruits. Villagra had sent Maldonado to ascertain Valdivia's wishes regarding the disposal and use of this force. The answer could not have been simpler. Maldonado was sent back posthaste to tell Villagra of the progress made in his absence and to instruct him to cross the Andes and come south with all the speed at his command.

Valdivia had left the fort on the Cautín unfinished. Pedro de Villagra carried on the work until he had put it into comfortable shape and made it adequate for defense. As soon as the weather permitted, he made a foray far afield with fifty men, leaving the balance of his forces within the fort. The expedition was successful in putting down several attempts at rebellion, and Pedro de Villagra had reason to believe that the area was definitely pacified. He reported on these activities to Valdivia who, his work in Concepción finished, left for the south in the first half of October, 1551.

Once he had joined Villagra, he made a number of

excursions into the surrounding country, and in January of 1552, he formally inaugurated the new city, naming it Imperial because of a two-headed eagle which appears to have been a usual design found on the roof beams of a number of native houses in the district.[6] The distribution of landed estates was postponed until further reconnaissance could be made of the surrounding country, but seventy-five were finally assigned to their fortunate owners on April 16.

Enthusiasm for this part of the country knew no bounds. Owners of estates in Santiago now wished to change them for others in the south, where vegetation was permanent, water abundant, and labor existed on a really vast scale. We may conclude with Encina that had the Araucanians been merely of the same caliber as *Picunches* and *Huilliches*, then it is likely that the center of gravity of Chile would have shifted from Santiago to the area which the Spaniards settled in the early 1550's. It was the Araucanians' stubborn resistance which gave Santiago some three hundred years' start, too large a handicap for the south ever to overcome.

12

The Transandine Province of Chile

We have recounted Maldonado's arrival in Chile with the news that Francisco de Villagra had completed his mission to Peru, and was now back at the latitude of Santiago, but awaiting instructions before crossing over to the west side of the Andes.

When Villagra left Chile for Peru, Valdivia had instructed him to return by way of Tucumán and to take possession of that part of the Chilean territory which lay east of the Andes but within the theoretical boundary of one hundred leagues from the shores of the Pacific. Villagra, however, was confronted with the difficulty that La Gasca had given an overlapping assignment to another Captain, Juan Nuñez de Prado, who had authority to undertake precisely the conquest of Tucumán.

After managing to raise a loan of 50,000 *Castellanos*, Villagra had small difficulty in attracting to his command a substantial force of well-equipped men, something which in itself was an indication of the considerable improvement in Chile's reputation since the days of Valdivia's early dilemma. Arrived in the valley of Sococha, Villagra commissioned his uncle Gabriel to contact in Cotagaita an additional force of some sixty or seventy recruits who had undertaken to join him there.

Nuñez de Prado had in the meanwhile set out for Tucumán with sixty men, but had left one of his captains, Juan de Santa Cruz, in Cotagaita for exactly the same purpose as that for which Gabriel de Villagra was now approaching. Santa Cruz had managed to recruit some thirty men, most of them presumably from Villagra's promised contingent, when on June 24, 1550, Gabriel attacked him with twice this number and took most of his men and all his supplies and left him to make his way back to Lima as best he could. Gabriel then joined Francisco in Jujuy, and the combined force, now some two hundred strong, continued southward.

Nuñez de Prado had himself already reached Tucumán where, at the end of July, he founded the city of El Barco. While on an expedition in the surrounding country, he had word of the appearance of a party of Spaniards in the neighboring village of Thomogasta. His understanding from his interpreters was that this group consisted of not more than eleven men, and he accordingly decided to fall upon them at night and oblige them to join his own command.

The intended victims were actually 110 in number under Francisco de Villagra himself, who for convenience had divided his large force into two halves which were proceeding south on different routes at some distance from each other. At midnight on November 10, Nuñez de Prado launched his attack and achieved at all events a partial surprise, which put Francisco de Villagra in some danger of his life. Villagra's greatly superior numbers, however, inevitably made themselves felt after the initial confusion, and Prado was forced to flee, practically alone, while his men surrendered to Villagra.

Villagra, much against the advice of his followers, sent a pardon to Nuñez de Prado, who accordingly returned and in at least well-feigned penitence presented his sword to his conqueror and bid him cut off his head with it for the wrong he had done him. Villagra returned the sword but, in allowing him to remain in charge of El Barco, obliged him to swear loyalty to Valdivia and to recognize the territory as coming within the boundaries of Chile.

The effects were short-lived. Nuñez de Prado, appointed Governor for the King by La Gasca, had small relish for being reduced to Lieutenant Governor for Pedro de Valdivia, and no sooner was Francisco de Villagra known to have crossed the Andes (September, 1551) than he obliged the citizens of El Barco, greatly against their will and with obvious loss of all their labor to date, to uproot themselves and refound their city in Calchaqui, territory which Nuñez de Prado conceived to be beyond one hundred leagues from the Pacific shores and consequently outside Valdivia's jurisdiction.

The news of these events up to the time of Villagra's departure from El Barco was contained in his report brought by Maldonado to Valdivia in May, 1551, and no doubt amplified by Maldonado himself, who had been an eye-witness of all that had taken place. Valdivia judged the position to be quite unsatisfactory and determined to have one of his own men as his representative in his eastern province. Francisco de Aguirre in La Serena seemed the best placed for his purpose, both geographically and by reason of the complete pacification of the territory under his command, which left him free from anxiety for what he already held and gave him assured lines of communication and supply.

Accordingly Valdivia called him down to Concepción, and

on October 8, 1551, he incorporated the territory of El Barco within the jurisdiction of La Serena, thus deposing Nuñez de Prado. These measures in effect remained inoperative for over a year, since Aguirre was for some time unable, for lack of sufficient men, to form the expedition necessary to take over this theoretical addition to his territory.

Valdivia returned to this matter in November of 1552. On the 14th of this month he re-enacted Aguirre's title to the eastern province, but also went considerably further. Not only did he confirm him in the position of Lieutenant Governor, responsible directly to Valdivia himself and independent of any subjection to the Lieutenant General, Francisco de Villagra, but added the provision that in the event of Valdivia's death, he was to remain as Governor of Tucumán and La Serena and be independent of any nominee who might succeed Valdivia in the governorship of the rest of the Chilean territory.

Aguirre's hitherto abortive attempts to mount an expedition to Tucumán were now greatly helped by the arrival overland of a force of approximately 110 men recruited and led down by Martin de Avendaño y Velasco, brother-in-law of Marshall Alonso de Alvarado. This welcome addition arrived in November, 1552, and a part of it was used to make good Aguirre's deficiency. As a result, he was enabled to set out in the same month to take possession of his new territory.

Aguirre met with no difficulty in crossing the Andes, presumably by the pass of San Francisco, but he naturally failed to find El Barco where Villagra had reported having left it. Nor, however, did he find it in Calchaqui, where we last heard of it.

It appears that a bad fire, poor crops, and frequent assaults by the natives had reduced the unfortunate Nuñez de Prado to despair of his new site, and the only solution he could find was to make another move. In June, 1552, he had accordingly made his third attempt in the province of Juries. The site selected on this occasion soon proved to be inappropriate, and a few more months found him making plans for a fourth attempt at a place called Taquitingasta, plans heartily resisted by the now thoroughly demoralized inhabitants of the wandering town. Nuñez de Prado, however, evidently a man of character if not a gifted leader, was determined to impose this last attempt on his recalcitrant followers, and his plans were on the point of completion when in May, 1553, the unfortunate settlement was set upon by Francisco de Aguirre's forces and forced to surrender to the new Lieutenant Governor. On the 21st of the same month, the *Cabildo* and populace accepted Aguirre's credentials as Valdivia's lieutenant, no doubt obtaining some small comfort from a fond hope that their long wanderings had now come to a definite conclusion.

Nuñez de Prado was himself absent at the time of Aguirre's arrival. By Aguirre's orders, he was arrested on his way back and sent off to Chile. "Tie me up and do what you like with me," he is reported to have said to some of his friends, in misery and disgust at the final outcome of his somewhat pathetic endeavors to overcome the difficulties of an enterprise for which, as Encina aptly puts it, he had not been born.

The ruthlessness of Aguirre's character soon made itself felt. Twenty of the more recalcitrant citizens were promptly packed off to Peru, together with the only two priests in the colony. Not until after Aguirre's arrest by Don Garcia Hurtado de Mendoza four years afterwards was the town able to obtain replacements for its banished clergy.

Aguirre, however, could at least agree with Nuñez on one

matter. He also decided to move the town from the site on which he had found it. The new selection was on the river Dulce, and perhaps to remove its unfortunate past associations, he took the occasion to change its name to Santiago del Estero.

On December 23, 1553, two days before Valdivia's death, Aguirre committed an act for which he has been greatly condemned, not least by Crescente Errazuriz. He wrote to the King, and obliged the *Cabildo* of Santiago del Estero to write also, asking for the segregation from Chile of the eastern province and, by implication, of the territory of La Serena also. "The said Governor [Pedro de Valdivia is understood], if your Majesty pleases, wishes it so and so declares in the dispatch which he gave me that if your Majesty be so gracious I shall be granted the governorship of this province." Errazuriz denounces this as rank disloyalty aggravated by falsehood.

While we have deferred conistently to Errazuriz's opinions on many points of controversy, opinions based on an exhaustive and scholarly examination of the available evidence, we believe that in the present instance he has gone further than the known facts warrant. In the edict confirming Aguirre's appointment to take over the eastern province issued in November, 1552, it will be remembered that Valdivia had rather surprisingly stated that, in the event of his death, Aguirre should continue as Governor of La Serena and Tucumán with complete independence from Valdivia's successor in the government of the rest of Chile. This is at least a very strong indication of the direction of his thoughts, and we have no evidence to prove that he may not have gone even further in conversation or in correspondence with Aguirre. If to this we add the fact that Aguirre categorically states that "the said Governor wishes it and so declares in the *dispatch which he gave me,"* then we appear to be moving on to even firmer ground, for if Aguirre had not had the dispatch he mentions, his statement, written without any knowledge of Valdivia's death and indeed two days before it occurred, would have had fatal consequences for him. Little as we admire Aguirre's arbitrary and ruthless character, we feel that he must have had some solid basis both for his request and for the grounds on which he prefers it. If the conclusion which we have drawn from the known facts is still not the whole truth, at all events those known facts are, in our opinion, quite insufficient to justify the unqualified condemnation to which Aguirre has been subjected by Errazuriz.

13

Further
Expansion
Southward

We have recounted Valdivia's leaving Concepción for the fort on the Cautín in October of 1551, the naming of this new foundation as the town of Imperial in January, 1552, and finally the distribution of the surrounding territory among seventy-five inhabitants on April 16 of the same year. In between these events Valdivia was far from idle.

Leaving Pedro de Villagra in charge of the young settlement shortly to be called Imperial, Valdivia set out with 150 Spaniards and numerous Indians auxiliaries at the beginning of November, 1551. The ever faithful ecclesiastic, Rodrigo Gonzalez de Marmolejo, was again a member of the party.

The first obstacle was the river Toltén, the southern boundary of the Araucanian territory proper, a formidable barrier in itself and seeming especially so on the present occasion because a large number of natives were stationed on the far bank and appeared to be ready to defend it against a landing. They were in fact, though the Spaniards were as yet unaware of the difference, merely *Huilliches*, who were to show even less taste for serious resistance than their *Picunche* cousins, who had already succumbed in the territory north of the Itata.

Preparing a number of rafts, Valdivia and his men crossed over, leading their swimming horses by the bridles. The fierce current took them swiftly downstream away from their Indian opponents, who were too astonished or too lethargic to follow them and oppose their safely gaining the southern bank.

Exploration was continued on the far side as far as Malafquen and the Pucón valley, where Villarrica was shortly to be founded. The *Huilliches* attempted a number of minor attacks which were easily beaten off.

News obtained from the natives in regard to silver mines in the mountains had a heartening effect, and Jeronimo de Alderete was sent with a small force to obtain confirmation. He returned with a satisfactory report and samples of a rich find.

Pedro de Villagra must have had some reason of which we are ignorant to fear for Valdivia's safety in the densely populated territory which he was now exploring, for he suddenly left Imperial with a force of seventy men to join his chief. They met near the river Callecalle, close to the site of the future town of Valdivia.

The soldiers' satisfaction with the part of the country they were now in increased every day. South of the Toltén was the pure *Huilliche* territory, the part of Chile which with its lakes, its unrivaled trout fishing, and magnificent scenery draws tourists from all over the world today. The civilization of the *Huilliches* was of the old *Chincha-Chilena* period[1] and, though perhaps decadent, was still greatly superior to that of the fighting Araucanians living between the Itata and the Toltén. All the Spaniards' descriptions are enormously enthusiastic, as well they might be from men who found themselves suddenly in possession of what is unquestionably one of the loveliest regions on earth.

It was near the Callecalle, in the valley of Mariquina, that Valdivia received in November, 1551, the news of Francisco de Villagra's safe arrival in Chile after crossing the Andes. Valdivia's satisfaction at the prospect of having a further two hundred men at his disposal knew no bounds, and he resolved to remain where he was until Villagra could join him. He spent the interval in constructing light shelters for his troops and resting them, though Jeronimo de Alderete was sent out with some fifty men to explore the surrounding country.

In order to follow the adventures of Nuñez de Prado and the further fortunes of the citizens of El Barco, we left Francisco de Villagra at the point where he had installed Nuñez as Valdivia's Lieutenant Governor in Tucumán. After leaving El Barco, Villagra continued to explore the country southward and by March, 1551 had reached Cuyo, just south of the present city of Mendoza. On May 18 he wrote his report to Valdivia, announcing his position and asking for instructions. We have seen this report reach Valdivia by Maldonado's hands in June, and Maldonado in due course took back the reply bidding him join Valdivia as soon as possible, but also not to lose the opportunity of exploring the route known as the "Inca Highway."

In its northern part this was, of course, the road originally used by Diego de Almagro, who had, however, crossed into Chile by the pass of San Francisco at the level of Copiapó. Francisco de Villagra had continued to come south on the east side of the Andes and was now to follow over the mountains the route which, so far as we know, his messenger Maldonado had been the first European to use. This followed the Uspallata valley and, from the old name *Puente del Inca,* which still exists there, seems certainly to have been the route principally used by the Peruvian imperialists.

Two misfortunes befell Villagra before he effected the crossing. The company under the command of his uncle Gabriel was assailed by a storm of such fury that two hundred of his native auxiliaries lost their lives of cold and fatigue. Not long afterward, a fire destroyed all the temporary shelters which Villagra had constructed to protect his own men while waiting for the spring weather, protection necessary to ensure reasonable safety in the mountain passes. Most of the army's supplies and several horses were lost in this disaster.

The expedition was immediately in some danger of a major reverse from exposure and lack of food. Gabriel de Villagra, however, in reminiscence of Diego de Almagro in the San Francisco pass some fifteen years previously, managed himself to effect a passage with eight men and secured the necessary help and supplies, which he brought back to the relief of the main force. The crossing was completed without further mishap late in September, 1551. Francisco de Villagra earned many tributes for his untiring exertions in attending to his men's welfare in their great difficulties. The satisfaction in Santiago at the arrival of this substantial addition to the colony's strength was as great as might be expected, and the *Cabildo* at once passed on the news to Valdivia, who, as already recorded, received it while marking time in the Mariquina valley.

After spending eight or ten days in Santiago, Villagra left his troops under the command of Gabriel and went south to join Valdivia.

Valdivia received his old friend with every manifestation of pleasure and satisfaction and as a reward for his services assigned him a magnificent estate in Imperial and several thousand Indians. At the same time he reappointed him his Lieutenant General.

Assuredly the firsthand account which he now received of his latest reinforcements did nothing to assuage Valdivia's impatience to continue the task of further expansion, and after a few days it was agreed that Villagra should return to Imperial to await the arrival of his new troops from Santiago and accelerate their preparation for the tasks ahead. They arrived in two contingents under the command of Gabriel de Villagra and Francisco de Riberos respectively.

Villagra left for Imperial on December 3. On the same day the *Huilliches* decided to make a trial in force against the power of the invaders. They chose probably as unfortunate a moment as could have been selected, for the Spaniards had saddled their horses and were on the point of departing from their camp. Completely armed and ready for their journey, they immediately mounted and inflicted tremendous slaughter on their attackers; 2,500 Indians were left dead on the field. Two days later, Jeronimo de Alderete returned from his expedition with the news that he also had disposed of a similar attack with the same disastrous result for the natives. These were the only serious attempts at resistance ever offered by the *Huilliches*, who subsequently made sincere overtures for peace and thereafter not only passively accepted the Spaniards' domination but joined forces with them against the Araucanians. The similarity of this attitude with that of the *Picunches* and its striking contrast with that of the Araucanians is in itself, as is pointed out in the Appendix, a sufficient refutation of Barros Arana's conclusion that one homogeneous race lived between Coquimbo and the Gulf of Reloncavi.

Meeting with no other opposition than that offered by the various rivers, Valdivia continued his march southward. The river Las Cruces caused the death of one soldier, and our old friend Gonzalez de Marmolejo is recorded as having also been within an ace of losing his life at the same place. A skirmish with the natives here was of minor importance, and Valdivia soon afterward made his camp on the site which was to be selected for the foundation of a further settlement. An expedition down the Callecalle river to the present position of Corral brought back news of what was described as the "best port in the world," being in fact the bay originally named after Valdivia by Bautista de Pastene in one of his early voyages.

The Governor now officially gave his own name to the town which still bears it, and in February, 1552, the Tree of Justice (a polite term always used on these occasions for the gallows without which no town was complete) was erected, and the *Cabildo* formed and sworn in.

No sooner had this latest settlement been founded than Villagra arrived with the whole of his force from Imperial. Many of his principal officers were among those who received lands in the area coming within the jurisdiction of the new town. In all, seventy estates were distributed.

Not content with this, Valdivia sent Alderete to found a further city in the Pucón valley, away from the sea and nearer to the mountains. Alderete chose a site near Lake Mullalauquen. Here the crossing of the Andes presented few difficulties, and the town was in fact directly on the route which in later years was used by the Viceroyalty of Buenos

Aires for reinforcements coming from Spain to take part in the Araucanian wars. It was named Villarrica from the large number of gold and silver mines which, with only moderate truth, the natives alleged to exist in the district. Forty estates were distributed.

The Governor himself, meanwhile, was continuing to press southward and using to the full that part of the season which still remained. In his letter to Charles V dated October 26, 1552, he says, "This past summer I came within 150 leagues of it," referring to the Straits of Magellan.[2] He adds that, keeping to the central valley between sea and mountains, he reached as far south as 42°. Taking 17½ Spanish leagues to one degree of latitude, Valdivia's two statements fit together as closely as can be reasonably expected and are sufficient to identify the furthest point south which, in fact, he was ever to gain. He says that at this extreme part of his march he was unable to proceed further because of a "fast-flowing river more than a mile wide, and so I went up river to the hills, and there I found a lake from which the river flowed and which in the opinion of all those who were with me had a perimeter of more than forty leagues." Undoubtedly this lake was the Gulf of Reloncavi, and the river the Chacao Canal, the island of Chiloe being mistaken as the southern bank of the supposed river.

Returned from Reloncavi, Valdivia went to Concepción, where he spent a large part of the winter busying himself with plans for an expedition to the Straits the following summer. On October 17 he was in Santiago giving final instructions to Jeronimo de Alderete, whom he had decided to send to Spain, principally for the purpose of trying to accelerate more direct recognition of his services in the form of at least some of the rewards for which he had already petitioned his monarch. To pay the expenses of Alderete's journey, Valdivia was obliged to sell his estate and town house in Santiago. The royal officials purchased the latter to provide accommodation for the *Cabildo,* the prison, the Royal Mint, and the State Treasurey.

Alderete set out at the end of October. He was accompanied by Diego Nieto de Gaete, Valdivia's brother-in-law, who was taking home 7,500 *Castellanos* to Doña Marina and was also entrusted with the mission of bringing her out to Chile. She was to spend the rest of her life in the new country which her husband had created and in which he had already died before she reached it.

14

The
Road
to
Tucapel

By his almost every action after returning from Peru, Valdivia was most industriously contriving his own death and destruction. Every step he took was down the road which led unerringly to Tucapel.

He has been most harshly condemned for providing the Araucanians with the only opportunity which could be of real avail to them, that of being able, after concentrating their own forces, to crush the Spanish contingents in detail. The justice of the charge in the light of subsequent events is irrefutable, but in the more limited light of all that could be known to Valdivia, a more moderate judgment should be accepted.

In the overriding cause of his destruction, he must undoubtedly be accorded a large measure of blame. The Spanish Court's injunction to put a term to further conquest and to consolidate what was already held almost certainly must have reached him. In his ambitious resolve to extend his province to the Magellan Straits and so to anticipate the claims of possible rivals, he paid no heed. Nothing can relieve him of this fundamental aspect of his responsibility.

Two factors must, however, be emphasized in his favor. Firstly, his critics feel none of the pressures to which Valdivia was subjected by his followers. To consolidate what he held at any given point inevitably required the recruitment of more Spaniards to his command. On the one hand to satisfy the demands of the veterans, and on the other to attract new-comers to what was always a laborious and hazardous enter-prise, he constantly required more land and native labor, and townships to act as centers for their defense. In other words, the work of consolidation itself became a prime factor in the process of expansion.

Secondly, it is possible to see causes very clearly now, because we have the advantage of being able also to examine their effects. The military prowess of the Araucanians did not reveal itself in its full significance until the actual day on which Valdivia lost his life to it. He took a calculated risk, a not unjustifiable risk in the light of all his experience. If his calculations were at fault, it was because he did not know, nor could he know, that one of the most remarkable of the world's savage races was quietly making preparations to fight as he had never seen savages fight before.

It was the unfortunate combination of these several factors which led to the dispersal of the Spanish forces among an ever-growing number of cities, in itself a big incentive to the Araucanian preparations for revolt. It was due to the same unfortunate combination that in the last two years of his life Valdivia appeared to do everything posssible to ensure that, when the need to go to Tucapel arose, he would be obliged to march with a quite inadequate handful of men who were all that he was able as a result of his own actions to gather together for a serious emergency.

The full extent of this dispersal of his forces is worth examining. Quite apart from the opening up of the towns in the south, he was concerned with taking possession of his trans-andine provinces. He entrusted these operations to three men:

Francisco de Aguirre in Tucumán, Francisco de Riberos in Cuyo, and Francisco de Villagra in the most southerly section as far as the Magellan Straits themselves.

Aguirre's movements we have already recounted. We merely note here that his expedition was responsible for putting ninety men on the wrong side of the Andes for the purpose of what was to come.

Ribero's expedition did not in fact eventuate, because the help he hoped to receive from Panama suffered shipwreck on the way down. Nevertheless, Valdivia had given him twenty-five men, and as a result, these men were in Santiago at the critical moment instead of being at Valdivia's disposal in the south.

Villagra had taken a total of sixty-five men from Concepción, and in December, 1552, crossed the Andes and marched southward toward the Straits. He was finally halted by a river which he found too big to cross, perhaps the Rio Negro, and made his return journey on the western slopes of the Andes. It was a sign of the times, for those who could read it, that while the natives left him unmolested on his journey away from the territory, they attacked him constantly on his way back.

This particular expedition was in fact concluded before the ultimate crisis arose and in itself had no direct effect upon it except insofar as it may have contributed to encourage the natives in their secret preparations. Villagra was, however, sent on another expedition not long after returning from this one, and the point to note is that he and his sixty-five soldiers were many leagues beyond recall when their presence might have made the whole difference.

Another source of loss was the departure of Don Martin de

Avendaño with thirty of the troops he had brought down with him. To this arrogant Spaniard, the granting of an estate which Valdivia had originally reserved for himself seemed a poor reward for the hardships of living beyond the pale of civilization. He returned to Peru after what appears to have been a quarrel with Valdivia.[1]

The attacks on Villagra's homeward march were not the only signs of the coming storm. In the Concepción area, the natives of several estates forced their Spanish masters to abandon them and took possession of their livestock and friendly slaves. One Spaniard was killed in these affrays.

The most serious outbreak, however, was on the island of Pucureo, the Governor's own property. The natives attacked the small fortress which had been constructed there and killed Alonso de Moya, who was in charge of the garrison of fourteen Spaniards. They would probably have overcome the rest of the garrison also had not word of the trouble reached Francisco de Villagra just after his arrival in Imperial from the first of his two expeditions noted above, enabling him to go to the rescue.

Villagra desired to end the trouble by peaceful means. He therefore tactfully pretended to believe that those reponsible for the attack were from the mountains, and offered a free pardon to all the local Indians who had incontinently fled after the relief of the Spanish garrison. The chieftains accepted this gambit, and the natives began to return to the island, bringing with them wood and forage. Their aims, however, were treacherous, for they used this means of introducing their weapons within the enemy's gates, while a larger gathering of warriors were concealed in the nearby forest for a frontal attack.

When the Indians inside the fort desired to make their

obeisance to Villagra in a body, he prudently refused and obliged them to pass before him one at a time. His soldiers, observing their leader's caution and becoming suddenly suspicious and alert, surprised one of the natives withdrawing his bow and arrows from a bundle of hay. The Spaniards wasted no further time and soon had the natives overpowered.

Contrary to the advice of his followers, who considered a mass killing to be the only fitting answer to this exhibition of treachery, Villagra contented himself with executing a few of the most culpable of the chieftains. Three or four days later he left the island, which had returned to a peaceful and normal state.

On arriving in Concepción, whither he had gone from Pucureo in order to give Valdivia an account of his mission to the south, Villagra found the inhabitants there possessed with the fever of a gold rush, the Governor among them. Gold washings in some abundance had been discovered between Concepción and Imperial, as also some rich mines in the neighborhood of Concepción itself. These facts are attested by Gongora Marmolejo and Mariño de Lobera alike. When a large pan of the precious metal was shown to Valdivia, he is said to have exclaimed in gratified astonishment, "Now indeed I begin to be a lord!"[2]

Experienced Spaniards came down from Santiago to organize the workings, and large numbers of natives began to be enlisted under them. Nevertheless, Valdivia adopted certain measures to protect the Indians from the worst excesses of exploitation and in particular prohibited any estate owner from putting more than ten per cent of his slaves to work in the mines.

The conglomeration of large numbers of natives in the

exacting labor of mining, which they detested, in itself constituted a danger, and in October, 1553, Valdivia established a
mining center at Quilacoya and set up a small garrison there. It
was at this period also that he created the forts of Arauco,
Tucapel, and Puren and manned them with twelve soldiers
apiece.

It was for the purposes of consolidation also, and not
primarily as a part of his plan to extend his conquests, that
Valdivia founded at this period the city of Los Confines, so
called because it was built on the boundary between the limits
of Concepción and Imperial. The present town of Angol lies
close to the original site of Los Confines.

Valdivia now made the three final and decisive contributions to his own destruction. They consisted of a further land
expedition by Francisco de Villagra, as already noted, a sea
expedition under Francisco de Ulloa, and the sending of Pedro
de Villagra to investigate the alleged existence of some salt
mines on the east side of the Andes.

Villagra and Ulloa left Concepción for the town of Valdivia
in the middle of September, 1553. Their two expeditions were
intended as far as was practicable to be mutually complementary, and a part of their mission was to select a site for a
further town in the neighborhood of what is now Osorno.

On October 27 or 28, Ulloa sailed from Valdivia with one
large and two small vessels. On November 8 he was in the Gulf
of Ancud, and on the 21st reached the Straits of Magellan with
one vessel, presumably the largest. He entered the Straits, but
did not go through to the Atlantic. He made his way safely
back to the fort of Valdivia on a date which must have been
very close to that of the Governor's death.

Francisco de Villagra himself set out in early November

and was still on his way back when the blow fell at Tucapel. He had sixty-five invaluable men with him. It is not known how many went with Pedro de Villagra to investigate the salt mines.

The coincidence of the maximum dispersal of the Spanish forces with the greatest concentration of their own must have made the Indians feel that some auspicious design was shaping their destinies. Their satisfaction appears to have been reflected in that insolence which invariably betrayed them. Valdivia undoubtedly began to be impressed, for in early December we find him sending Gabriel de Villagra with a few soldiers to reinforce Imperial, and Diego de Maldonado with four men to perform a like service in Tucapel. The adventures of this last group mark the beginning of the rebellion proper.

Maldonado reached the fort of Arauco safely, but in the second stage of his journey between Arauco and Tucapel he was fiercely attacked, and three of his four men were killed. With the fourth he succeeded in regaining Arauco.

Meanwhile the symptoms of Indian behavior were sufficiently alarming at Puren to cause Alonso Coronas, in charge of the fort there, to take some of the native chieftains into custody. According to Lobera, he roasted them on hot grills to extract the truth from them regarding the Indians' plans for a general attack, which was now being freely rumored. The natives gave away nothing, but neither did they remove the Spaniards' anxiety. Coronas sent messages to the Governor, expressing his concern at the situation, and to Imperial, asking for reinforcements.

Other and far more serious reasons for the concern were soon apparent. At Tucapel the natives repeated the stratagem which had failed at Pucureo. A number entered the gates of the fort with loads of hay in which they had hidden their weapons and attempted a surprise attack at close quarters. The Spaniards succeeded in driving them out, but after sustaining some sharp encounters with more numerous forces, they felt in insufficient strength to wait for relief and withdrew to combine with the garrison at Puren. The fort at Tucapel was promptly sacked and burned by the natives.

Meanwhile Imperial had taken heed of the call from Coronas. Juan Gomaz de Almagro, possibly attracted by the accounts of the rich finds of all kinds in the south, had just reached Imperial from Santiago, where he had left both an estate and the office of mayor. The City Council asked Gomez, in the absence of Pedro de Villagra, to go to the help of Puren with such men as they could spare, amounting to not more than six. The size of this reinforcement in itself demonstrates the pathetic weakness of the towns, not only too widely dispersed to be of immediate assistance to each other in the event of attack, but now individually debilitated by the drain made upon them by the various expeditions which were on foot in all directions.

Gomez at once accepted the commission, and on his arrival at Puren found that the garrison which had withdrawn from Tucapel had already provided a welcome reinforcement. He accepted the post of commander-in-chief of the combined contingents.

Three days later the natives appeared in force. Twelve thousand is the figure commonly given in contemporary sources, though it must be treated with the usual reserve. What is clear is that the first battalions of a very large native concentration had now been put into the field.

Gomez made a sortie with seventeen Spaniards and doubtless also a substantial number of Indian auxiliaries, who are, however, almost as though by conspiracy, never mentioned in contemporary accounts. The Spaniards made three separate charges, but were unable to break the Indians, who were now opposing serried ranks of spears to their onslaughts and making excellent use of their clubs at close quarters. After losing two horses and having several men wounded, Gomez withdrew into the fort. He had unquestionably suffered a defeat.

After sending appeals for further help to Imperial and Los Confines by means of friendly Indians, who appear to have been reliable for this kind of service, Gomez decided to make a further attempt to break the enemy formations. On this occasion he was successful, and the Indians, turning in flight, were chased off the field by the Spanish horse.

Gomez lost no time in advising Valdivia of the change in his fortunes, and for the purpose sent a Spaniard to convey the news. Antonio Diaz has recorded Valdivia's pleasure on receiving the good tidings.[3]

Meanwhile the Indian messenger sent to Imperial had accomplished his mission, and Pedro de Avendaño was promptly dispatched with a further fourteen soldiers. He reached Puren some three days after the Indian withdrawal, raising the total strength to about thirty men.

On December 19, Gomez received a letter of reply from the Governor. Valdivia was not content to see Tucapel abandoned (his own estate of Pucureo was in the area, but the suggestion that this was more than a minor consideration is unworthy), and he instructed Gomez to meet him there on Christmas Day with the largest number of soldiers he could spare without endangering Puren itself. He emphasised this last consideration by mentioning it twice in the letter, according to a witness who actually heard Gomez read it aloud.[4]

Though the Indians had now entirely disappeared from the neighborhood of Puren, this could not be safely interpreted as anything but a sign that they were gathering for another attack. Gomez was begged by his senior men not to leave for Tucapel, on the grounds that if he took an adequate force with him, Puren would be left as weak as it was before Avendaño's arrival from Imperial and quite incapable of resisting the heavier pressure which it was now confidently expected would be exerted against it. Gomez, however, sternly rejected these not unreasonable entreaties. He had express instructions to meet Valdivia in Tucapel, and nothing would stop him from making arrangements for these instructions to be carried out.

At ten o'clock on the night of December 24, he and fourteen men were in the saddle and on the point of leaving the fort, when the guard brought in an Indian who had been caught observing what was going forward and was suspected of being a spy. Under examination the Indian stated that in the neighboring woods were no less than seventeen Araucanian levies, amounting in all to some thirty thousand men, who were preparing to attack the fort before dawn. Gomez could not resist the force of such news as this and instantly cancelled his departure.

The night passed without incident. The sentinel reported having seen large numbers of native warriors flitting among the trees, but if this was something more than imagination excited by nervous tension, those warriors had had bigger game in view and had left Puren undisturbed. Next day Gomez rode out over the surrounding country and found no signs anywhere of the enemy. Though his decision to remain in Puren had been more than defensible in the light of the evidence which was available when he made it, nevertheless it now weighed heavily on him, and he determined to leave for

Tucapel that same night. Valdivia was fighting for his life while Gomez was indulging in these reflections, and was almost certainly already dead when the latter left Puren to meet him.

Leaving Avendaño in charge of the remaining garrison, Gomez set out with thirteen Spaniards. Traveling all night over difficult country, he was within some ten miles of Tucapel before any signs of the Araucanians became apparent. At Ilicura he found large bands of Indians who made light attacks on him, but for the most part contented themselves with insulting him at a distance and telling him to give up hope and to surrender, since the Governor and his whole force had been overcome and slaughtered.

The Spaniards, accustomed to Indian boastfulness which was designed to reduce the morale of their enemies, at first paid little heed. A growing uneasiness, however, began to grip them as they proceeded. There was no sign anywhere of any Spaniards but themselves. If Valdivia were really close at hand, surely he would be attacking this large concentration of Indians, who would themselves in that case be more concerned to avoid being taken between two Spanish detachments than to boast of past achievements.

Anxiety gave way to fear and finally to sickening certainty. As the Spaniards approached the fort, several Indians exhibited trophies which told only too plain a story. Spanish weapons were displayed by some, while others had dressed themselves in the clothes of their fallen foes. There could no longer be the smallest doubt that a disaster of the first order had occurred.

15

The
Death
of
Pedro de Valdivia

It will be recalled that Alonso Coronas, in command at Puren, had become extremely concerned at the mounting signs of a general uprising and had sent a report on the situation to the Governor in Concepción.

This report reached Valdivia in the first half of December. He could now no longer ignore the growing evidence of a widespread native conspiracy, and he determined, as he later advised Gomez, to go himself to Tucapel and to take matters in hand personally.

It was no easy matter, however, owing to arrangements for which he himself was entirely responsible, to raise a respectable force. The expeditions had drained the towns of all but the minimum numbers required for essential defense purposes, and the forts were all in the position of needing rather than being able to supply reinforcements. It was only with some difficulty that Valdivia was able to raise a force of fifty men to accompany him.

His first objective was the mining center at Quilacoya, where he spent approximately one week. Rumors of insurrection and the difficulty of obtaining reinforcements had alarmed the soldiers there, and to ensure an adequate defense which would restore the morale of this important post, Valdivia threw up a small fort and left several members of his own force to augment the garrison. It was from here also that he wrote his letter to Gomez bidding him meet him in Tucapel on December 25. Valdivia left Quilacoya for Arauco on December 19.

The weight of the evidence goes to show that Valdivia had forty men in the fight at Tucapel. We must suppose, therefore, that in addition to leaving a few at Quilacoya, he left a few more at Arauco. As usual, however, there is no record of the number of Indian auxiliaries he had with him; this may have been considerable.

It was an Indian who had once been a Spanish auxiliary who was now preparing the trap into which Valdivia was being drawn. He was no other than a youth who had at one time been Valdivia's groom.

Lautaro, who had been known to the Spaniards as Alonso, is in some measure a legendary figure, though there can be absolutely no doubt either of his existence or of his extraordinary genius. Nothing is known of how or in what circumstances he left Valdivia's service. Even less is known of how a youngster of not more than twenty could have so impressed the Araucanian chieftains as to become commander-in-chief of their armies. So far as facts are concerned, we have to be content with the knowledge that he did so.

We can, however, legitimately surmise an outline of what occured. The Spaniards had now been under permanent observation by the Araucanians proper for about four years. All the traditional native tactics had failed and were clearly going to continue to fail. A very great united effort on a national scale presented the only possible solution, and this again could only succeed by the strict and disciplined application of new tactics. The extent of Lautaro's influence in bringing this thinking about must be conjectural.

In such a situation, however, it is possible to imagine a conflict of opinion between a number of practically autonomous chieftains, and a consequent tendency for a vigorous and single-minded youth of genius (he must be conceded the title) to gain the ascendancy. If we add to this that he had been in the service of Valdivia himself, had observed both him and other Spaniards at very close quarters, had heard intimate conversations which revealed their fears and weaknesses and not merely the outward invincibility which was all the other Araucanian chiefs had witnessed, then the causes of the ascendancy become even clearer. What is certain is that Lautaro finally succeeded in getting the management of the campaign into his remarkably capable hands.

It is not difficult to trace his plans. We have seen that concurrently with the growing cohesion of the Indians, the Spaniards had been almost recklessly dispersing their own forces. Spies were at work everywhere, and Valdivia's decision to go to Tucapel with a small force would be not only known but seized upon as a golden opportunity for striking the opening blow at the Governor himself.

Gomez's assignation for December 25, contained in a letter which was openly read aloud in Puren, was no secret, and we have observed the means taken by Lautaro to prevent his keeping that appointment: first came rumors of impending Indian attacks and finally, when these were unsuccessful, the appearance of a supposed Indian spy and his declaration that thirty thousand natives were preparing an onslaught before dawn. Gomez's consequent decision to postpone his departure then made it possible to move to Tucapel, during the night of December 24, the levies which would otherwise have been needed to prevent his joining forces with Valdivia.

The second part of the plan was to conceal all the available natives forces in the woods surrounding the fort at Tucapel and continually to close in and block the paths behind Valdivia as he advanced towards it. Finally a large number of tactically maneuverable battalions would be successively launched against the Spaniards until sheer exhaustion overcame them. Lautaro was supremely aware that Spaniards were as human as Araucanians, and that their horses, still something of a fearful mystery to the vast majority of the Indians, had perfectly well-defined limits to their endurance. Lautaro had not wasted his time as a groom.

On December 23, Valdivia set out from the fort at Arauco, and at the end of the day, without sighting any Indians, he reached Lavolebo, where he spent the night. From here he sent forward four soldiers to reconnoiter. They were trapped and killed by the natives who were watching every move.

Considerably disturbed by the failure of his four men to return, as they should have done during the night, Valdivia continued the march next day. Bands of Indians did now appear from time to time, but only in order to attract pursuit and lead the Spaniards closer to the trap.

Gongora Marmolejo relates that the severed arm of one of the missing four soldiers was found by the Spaniards at the side of their path. This gave the Governor pause, and he received no encouragement when his servant Agustinillo adjured him to "remember the night you fought at Andalien."[1] He was referring to the Spaniards' first real taste of the Araucanian quality, when they had in fact only narrowly escaped a severe defeat. However, the enthusiasm of the younger men of the party, and above all his engagement to meet Gomez, decided the Governor to go forward.

On December 25, he reached Tucapel, abandoned by its garrison two weeks earlier, and surveyed the ruins of the fort. There were no signs of any Indians, far less of Gomez de Almagro.

Suddenly out of the surrounding woods sprang the first Indian battalion and fell upon the invaders. Since no Spaniard survived the battle, what follows is largely traditional conjecture, though in its main lines probably substantially true. The story which Gongora Marmolejo obtained from an alleged Indian eyewitness named Don Alonso provides the mainstay of the account, which has also been legitimately influenced by the known Indian tactics at the subsequent battle of Mariguenu.

After recovering from the first shock, the Spaniards were able to form up and, placing their baggage in the rear, thundered down upon the Indians in one of their devastating charges. Fierce fighting then took place in which many Indians were killed and wounded. The Spaniards, however, and their horses inevitably sustained a certain amount of damage also. Suddenly the Indians withdrew and disappeared down into the gully, where they drank from the stream and rested while awaiting their next call to the fray. A momentary sensation of victory in the minds of the Spaniards was brusquely shattered by the emergence from cover of the second Indian battalion. Again the Spaniards charged; again there was more fierce fighting and again an Indian withdrawal with heavy losses. But they had taken their toll of the Spaniards, who were given no rest before the appearance of the third battalion. Valdivia led a charge of twenty-six horse on this occasion and eventually forced the Indians from the field, only to find himself faced with yet a further contingent as fresh as the first had been. Again Valdivia charged with every available man, but the Spaniards' impetus was failing, and this time they failed to break the Indian formation. Three Spaniards lay on the field.

The trumpets sounded recall. Valdivia turned to his men and asked, "Gentlemen, what shall we do?" Captain Altamirano, native of Medellin, replied, "What would your honor have us do but fight and die?"[2] Well may Valdivia have feared that to postpone his withdrawal any longer would be simply to aggravate the seriousness of what was already a decisive defeat. He nevertheless decided to throw in every man and horse in a last desperate attempt. The sweating and exhausted men and beasts broke before the stubborn ranks of completely fresh native warriors, and several more Spaniards were brought to the ground. Sounding his trumpets, Valdivia ordered an immediate retreat.

The long-planned moment had arrived for Lautaro to launch the whole of his reserves in a massed attack. After a brief resistance, it became a matter of every Spaniard for himself, and the butchery started. The Indians, not waiting to pillage the Spanish baggage as Valdivia had hoped, pursued their fleeing victims, whose horses were worn out and handicapped by the blocking of the paths which the natives had been careful to attend to. One by one the Spaniards were caught and done to death.

Thanks to his excellent mount, Valdivia himself, together with a priest called Pozo, managed to escape immediate capture. Their horses, however, were too exhausted to make headway over some marshy land in their path, and they were soon surrounded and taken. Valdivia, Pozo, and it would seem also the faithful servant Agustinillo all died together.

There are many versions of the manner of Valdivia's death. Since no Spanish eyewitness lived to tell the tale, there was plenty of scope for imaginative speculation. The *Cabildo* of Santiago, in their letter to the Royal Audience at Lima, state that he was tortured for three days before he expired, but there is not a shred of evidence to support this account. Mariño de Lobera feels the attraction of lending the story a classical flavor and says that the Indians killed Valdivia by obliging him to drink in molten form the gold he was so fond of making them labor to obtain for him. Gongora Marmolejo quotes his Indian informant, Don Alonso, as having witnessed the whole affair. According to this version, the natives stripped the Governor of everything but his helmet, which they were unable to unfasten. They then dragged him about a mile to a watering place, and with a ceremonial knife made a sea shell, they cut off his arms at the elbows and cooked and ate them in front of him. Agustinillo, who had in the meanwhile removed Valdivia's helmet, was then quartered, and Valdivia was despatched with a club after kissing a cross of two straws held up by Father Pozo.

The multiplicity of the versions is itself the best proof that nothing was in fact known at all. Valdivia may well have lost his life in the battle itself. Encina most rightly remarks that in any case the Indians would never have departed from the rules of the *admapu*[3] and that the most probable account is that given by some chieftains to Rosales. According to this version Valdivia was killed quite simply by the blow of a club, and his heart cut into small pieces which were eaten by the principal chieftains. This is as near to the truth as we are ever likely to attain.

So died the conqueror of Chile. "He was," says Gongora

Marmolejo, "fifty-six[4] years of age when he met his death, a man of good stature, of affable expression, and with a large head in keeping with his body which had become stout, broad-shouldered, and wide-chested. He was of good understanding and gracious in the granting of favors. On attaining high rank, it pleased him to give of what he had. He was generous in all things, liked to dress well and even splendidly, as he liked also others who did so. He was fond of good eating and drinking, and was friendly and human with everybody. But there were two things which clouded all these virtues: he hated men of noble birth, and he lived with a Spanish woman in concubinage, to which he was much addicted." This description was given by a man who knew him well and was serving in Chile at the time of his death.

The assessment of Valdivia's ranking in the galaxy of the *Conquistadores* is no easy matter. He has not achieved the renown of Cortés or Pizarro, but it is difficult to separate this from the fact that Chile did not provide the romantic background of a Mexico or a Peru. If we go below the surface, however, we must conclude that it is precisely because of this difference, not in spite of it, that Valdivia's claim to a place in the front rank is such a strong one.

Almagro had removed whatever glamor Chile may have derived from being unknown. When Valdivia attempted to attract recruits to his original expedition, they, in his own words, "fled from it as from the plague." There was no flourishing civilization, there were no magnificent buildings or temples, no roads or communications, and little enough gold. Cold wet weather and hard fighting were the only positive substance of the reports which Almagro's men brought back with them to Peru.

Yet Valdivia went, after determinedly overcoming almost insuperable difficulties in obtaining followers, finance, and even a clear title to the leadership of his own project. And he stayed in his apparently poor territory, of which only he in the beginning had the vision to see the real wealth and beauty, until he died there. Nor was this because his death was premature. It was his set resolve to live all his days in his new country. Not in one single action is there the faintest suggestion of any desire or intent to take from it whatever riches it might give him for the purpose of living in ease and comfort elsewhere. He had surmounted the limitations of the more common ambitions of his fellows when he renounced an enormous fortune in Peru, nor ever again did he give it even a backward glance.

According to his own account, written to Charles V not long before he died, he had spent 500,000 *Castellanos* of his own on the conquest, and was in debt to the tune of 200,000 more. "For," as he tells his sovereign in another place, "my interest is not to buy one palm of land in Spain, though I owned a million ducats, but to serve your Majesty with them and be given my reward in this land, that it may be enjoyed by my heirs after my days and that memory of me shall remain and of them thereafter."

Valdivia took nothing out of Chile for himself except certain relatively modest sums which he remitted to his wife as opportunity offered. The gold he obtained from his mines, and a good deal of his followers' gold also, was all devoted to the obtaining of supplies and reinforcements. And whereas he repaid his followers from his subsequent income, nobody ever repaid him. Granted that larger, more glittering prizes were always in prospect, there was never any attempt to hedge, or to take short cuts to obtain an early enjoyment of them. Capable of driving the shrewdest of bargains, and without losing for a moment his firm grip on the day-to-day administrative details of his designs, he combined this hardheadedness with an idealism which kept his vision constantly set on horizons well beyond his immediate reach. Without having any heir of his own body, it is of his heirs appointed and his heirs' heirs that he speaks when he asks his sovereign for rewards and favors. Here is no commonplace adventurer whose intimate thoughts reach us across the centuries.

His letters are a delight to read. They are colorful and vivid, racy in their description of action, and above all imbued with a very deep affection for the land he was discovering and molding to his purpose. In his letter of September 4, 1545, he gives a description of his new country which is as true now as on the day he wrote it and will echo in the hearts of all who have been fortunate enough to live there. "He (Alonso de Monroy) may tell the merchants and people if they wish to come and settle, to come. For this land is such that there is none better in the world for living in and for founding a family, and I say this because it is very open, very healthy, and altogether pleasing; it has only four months of winter, and in them it is only when the moon is at the quarter that it rains for a day or two; on all the other days the sun is so bright that there is no need to draw near the fire. Such pleasant breezes temper the summer's heat that a man can be out in the sun all day without suffering any ill effects. It is a land abundant in pastures and crops and for the yielding of every kind of livestock and plant imaginable, masses of fine timber for the building of houses and endless firewood for use in them, the mines most rich in gold, and indeed the whole land is full of it; and wherever men may wish to take it there they will find a place to sow, and the wherewithal to build, and water, wood, and grass for their cattle, so that it seems that God created it for the express purpose of having everything close at hand."

The reference to gold must be accounted an exaggeration, and we feel persuaded that Valdivia was here guilty of propaganda for outside consumption. New recruits were vital to him, and he knew, none better, that gold was the one really powerful enticement. The touch of unscrupulousness where the ends seemed to him to justify the means must be accepted in our final estimate of his character.

Doña Marina reached Chile not long after her husband's death and lived there for thirty-eight years. The five nephews whom she had brought with her and regarded as her sons were all lost in the Araucanian wars. She lived out her life modestly and was almost unknown to the generation which grew up while she was in the country. On April 12, 1592, her will was opened, and "Doña Marina Ortiz de Gaete, widow, wife that was of the Governor Don Pedro de Valdivia," named heirs to the chaplaincy which she had instituted for her own soul and for "the soul of Don Pedro de Valdivia." It was fifty-seven years since she had seen him for the last time, when she bid him good-bye in Spain as he set out for the Indies.

Hard and anxious times were in store for the colony after Tucapel. At Marigueñu two months later, Francisco de Villagra was to be decisively defeated with the loss of no less than eighty-eight Spanish lives out of a well-equipped force of 154. Concepción was immediately abandoned to the natives, and it seems probable that it was only the customary alcoholic celebration of their triumph that prevented the Araucanians from advancing in time to massacre the inhabitants during their slow retreat to Santiago.

Nor was Lautaro eventually defeated by the Spaniards so

much as by drought, famine, and disease. The large concentration of warriors had caused the Indians to neglect their crops, and they soon used up their meager reserves of food. Three dry seasons in succession immediately followed, and this, combined with the Spanish practice of deliberately destroying such crops as they found or could reach, led to famine and an epidemic of what appears to have been typhoid fever. It is estimated that the Araucanians may have lost a third of their entire population of some 400,000 individuals between 1554 and 1557.

Lautaro could not overcome so tremendous a handicap and was unable to follow up and take advantage of his initial successes. When he met his death at Peteroa in April of 1557, it was at the head of a force of not more than eight hundred Araucanian warriors, of whom nearly seven hundred died fighting. On this occasion, Francisco de Villagra certainly took ample revenge for his reverse at Marigueñu, but it is Lautaro who is sublime in defeat and death.

All these events, however, belong not properly here, but to another much longer story of a three hundred years' war. By the time Valdivia died, there was no real doubt that the Spaniards had come to stay, nor was there any further serious resistance outside the belt of the Araucanian territory proper. Chile had been founded, and those who love her magnificent scenery, superb climate, and active and warmhearted inhabitants will agree that few men in history have been fortunate to leave behind them so splendid a monument as it has been Valdivia's privilege to raise to his own "Fame and Memory," a reward which by its nature he could never enjoy, but the only one which held any real value for him.

The
Problem
of the
Araucanians

It was by no means the case, as we have seen, that the whole of what we now know as Chile was inhabited by this one remarkable people. It has in fact been stated on good authority that the descendants of no less than forty different races were living there when the Spaniards first invaded it. While it is no part of the writer's aim to deal in detail with this complex and specialized subject, a brief outline of the main racial pattern must nevertheless be attempted in order to put the problem of the Araucanians into perspective.

At the time of the invasion, the territory between Arica and the Gulf of Reloncavi was inhabited by five principal groups, apart from the fishing tribes on the coasts and the *Puelches* in the high Andine valleys. It was the fourth of these groups, counting from north to south, who put up the resistance which it took the Spaniards, and their Chilean descendants, nearly three and a half centuries and countless lives finally to overcome.

The most northerly of these five groups were the Atacamanians. They lived in the Andean valleys of the present provinces of Tarapacá and Antofagasta, where climatic con-

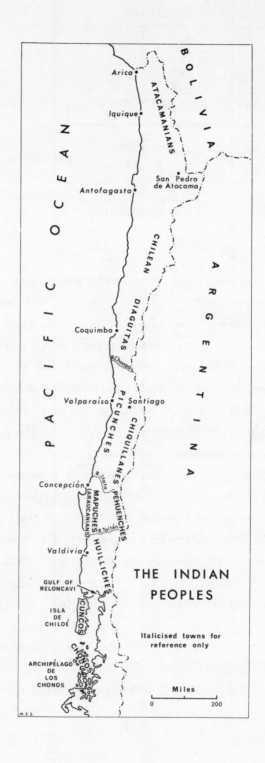

PACIFIC OCEAN

BOLIVIA

ARGENTINA

Arica

Iquique

ATACAMANIANS

San Pedro
de Atacama

Antofagasta

CHILEAN

DIAGUITAS

Coquimbo

R.Choapa

Valparaíso   Santiago

PICUNCHES

CHIQUILLANES

Concepción   R.Itata

MAPUCHES   PEHUENCHES

(ARAUCANIANS)

R.Toltén

HUILLICHES

Valdivia

GULF OF
RELONCAVI

ISLA
DE
CHILOÉ

CUNCOS

ARCHIPÉLAGO
DE
LOS
CHONOS

CHONOS

THE INDIAN
PEOPLES

Italicised towns for
reference only

Miles

0   200

M.E.S.

ditions were rather more propitious to life than they are today. Little is known of their origins, though it is believed that they may have been on Chilean soil for as much as two thousand years. They grew crops and tended their herds of llamas. They spun and wove the wool of these beasts, and had achieved some skill in basketwork and pottery. They spoke a language which was unrelated to that of any of their southern neighbors.

Separated from the Atacamanians by a long stretch of desert, a tribe whom Latcham called the Chilean *Diaguitas* inhabited the present provinces of Atacama and Coquimbo. They practiced terrace agriculture on hilly slopes and had some knowledge of metallurgy, making hoes, chisels, and other implements from bronze. Latcham excavated extensively in this territory some sixty to seventy years ago and made out a convincing case for the belief that these people shared a common ancestry with the Argentine *Diaguitas*, who had once occupied the provinces of Salta, Tucumán, and Santiago del Estero, among others. It is this which has given rise to their name. They too spoke a different language from that of their southern, as well as their northern, neighbors.

Continuing southward, the three other main groups lay between the river Choapa and the Reloncavi Gulf, consisting of the northern and southern branches of a race which appears at one time to have occupied the whole of this territory, and a separate and distinct race of intruders, the Araucanians, who had cut out a substantial wedge for themselves between the rivers Itata and Toltén. We are faced with the difficulty that the older race have never had any one name of national significance by which they can be referred to. The early writers mostly described them as *Indios de Chile*, qualifying this general term by some more strictly local denomination if they wished to particularize; e.g., the *Pencos*, the *Mapochinos*, the *Quillotanos*, and so forth.

The name *Araucano* has sometimes come to have almost this national significance, though misleadingly. Originally invented by Ercilla in the early days of the conquest, it was intended by him to refer only to the fighting race who form the subject of his poem *"La Araucana"*; i.e., that important middle group of the three with which we are dealing.

Latcham attempted to overcome this difficulty of nomenclature by recommending the permanent application of three indigenous names, namely *Picunche*, *Mapuche*, and *Huilliche*. While, as he says, they are not entirely appropriate, they are nevertheless of good Indian origin and have a large measure of historical sanction. They are a great deal more suitable than new inventions and have become generally adopted. An examination of the origin of these names is in order.

The Indian word *Mapuche* is made up of *mapu*, or land, and *che*, or people, and originally meant the people of the immediately surrounding territory. Every Indian from the river Choapa to the Gulf of Reloncavi was *Mapuche* to himself as were those living in his near neighborhood. To him all Indians outside this restricted area were *Pelum*, or strangers, though further distinguished by the direction from which they hailed. If from the north, they were *Picunche* (north people); if from the south, *Huilliche* (south people); if from the east, *Puelche* (eastern people). Thus to the Indians of the Santiago district, they were themselves the *Mapuche*, while those in Lampa, for example, were *Picunche* and those in Talagante were *Huilliche*. To the Talagante inhabitants, on the other hand, only they were *Mapuche,* while their neighbors around Santiago were *Picunche* and those in Rancagua were *Huilliche.*

By a not unnatural analogy, the three names have come to be applied to the three large groups of which we are writing The word *Huilliche* as applied to the southern group is sanctioned by usage from the early days of conquest. *Mapuche* is now quite generally applied to the remaining Indians in Araucanian territory, the descendants of the fighting race. *Picunche* was used by the Spaniards from the seventeenth century onwards to refer to the Indians north of the river Bío-Bío, and Latcham has merely made the slight change of substituting the river Itata for the Bío-Bío. All these three groups spoke the same language.

To complete the racial diagram, a few words must be said about the tribes lying to the east and south. Living in the high valleys on both sides of the Andes, more or less on a level with *Picunche* territory, was a race called the *Chiquillanes.* Little is known of them except that in the summer months they would descend from their mountain homes and trade or rob as circumstances permitted. From Chillán south another nomad race lived in the same sort of way as the *Chiquillanes.* These were known as *Pehuenches* from the fact that they inhabited a region covered in pine trees, or *pehuenes,* the cones of which were an element in their diet. In general the word *Puelches* (east people) was used to refer to these tribes.

To the south of the Reloncavi Gulf, the island of Chiloé was inhabited by the *Cuncos,* who formed the most southern part of the *Huilliche* group and spoke the same language. It is believed that the pressure southward caused by the Araucanian invasion was probably responsible for a part of this race going over to the island, where they appear to have displaced the *Chonos,* who were forced farther south still on to the archipelago which now bears their name. This is supported by the number of place names on the island ending in *ao, ac, ec,* and *uy;* for example, Abtao, Achao, Quenac, Laitec, Tenuy, Chincuy.

Farther south still, on the mainland and the island of Tierra del Fuego, were tribes such as the *Yahganes,* the *Caucahues,* and the *Alacalufes.* They are the remnants who have been pushed into the most uninhabitable parts of the continent, are dying out, and have contributed little if anything to the Chilean nation of today.

The superb and uncompromising defiance displayed by the Araucanians in the face of their European aggressors, not merely for a few years but for well over three centuries, is in such deep contrast with the almost immediate submission of their neighbors that there might be expected always to have existed a strong presumption of vital differences of blood and racial origin. The actual presumption was in fact for many years just the reverse.

At the time of the Spaniards' arrival, all the Chilean natives living between the river Choapa and the Gulf of Reloncavi were undoubtedly speaking the same language. This single fact induced Barros Arana to state categorically that they were all of one homogeneous race. Such was the prestige of this eminent Chilean historian that his assumption remained virtually unchallenged for more than half a century. To archaeology, and particularly to Ricardo Latcham, must be given the credit for calling it into question. Patient investigation has tended to vindicate the assertions, and more particularly the implications, contained in the humbler writings of the earlier chroniclers to the confusion of their more illustrious nineteenth-century successors.

Since archaeology first raised the problem which the tremendous authority of Barros Arana had somehow been sufficient to keep out of sight, the early chronicles and other contemporary documents have been freshly examined for further light. Their evidence, though entirely ignored by the nineteenth century writers, is formidable. A few outstanding examples will serve to show the extent to which they tend to corroborate what the archaeological discoveries have suggested.

In approximately 1485, the Peruvian Inca Huaina Capac proceeded to enlarge his domains south of Coquimbo, the then southern limit of the Empire as fixed by his father Tupac Yupanqui some twenty-five years before. His progress met no serious opposition until soon after the crossing of the river Maule, when he was offered battle by a large force of the warriors of that district. It is said that the battle lasted for two whole days without perceptible advantage to either side and was then inconclusively broken off. It has even been suggested that the Incas is fact sustained a severe defeat. Whichever of the versions is the true one, it is at least certain that the Incas laid no claim to a victory, and that they did not in fact ever advance south of the Maule again. For the next fifty years they fixed the southern limit of their Empire on the river Cachapoal, giving the name of *Promaucaes* ("rebellious people") to the Indians living farther south. They appear also, however, to have left a few garrisions between the Cachapoal and the Maule and to have treated this territory as a species of buffer state.

It is not impossible to suppose that the Araucanians took

part in this battle, in support of their northern neighbors, against a common enemy. The fact that the Incas never renewed their advance southward is strongly suggestive, when combined with the rest of the historical evidence, of this having indeed been the case; if so, it is the first recorded example of the respect which the Araucanians imposed upon those who came up against them in battle. More importantly, it provides the first indication from a chronological standpoint that the Indians to the south of Coquimbo were not by any means all of the same blood, but that a very unusual and surprising element had been introduced somewhere south of the Maule.

The second recorded instance of a display of the fighting qualities of this people is provided by their first meeting with the Spaniards. Diego de Almagro had advanced with his entire strength in 1536 as far as the Aconcagua valley. Here he paused, but, as we have seen, detached a force of one hundred men to explore the territory farther south under Gomez de Alvarado.

This expedition, like the Incas some fifty years previously, found no opposition worthy of mention before reaching the river Maule. Here a few groups of hostile Indians did offer some show of resistance, though it was not in any way sufficiently serious to test the Spanish strength. The advance continued without further difficulty as far as the river Itata, the northern border of the Araucanian territory proper.

At the juncture of the rivers Nuble and Itata, the battle of Reinoguelen took place. The Araucanians came into the attack in great masses, and while they did not at this first meeting with the strange new formidable cavalrymen appear yet to possess the discipline and organization which they displayed later, their dash and determination considerably disconcerted the Spaniards, who had hitherto met no Indians capable of any kind of sustained resistance to their horses and greatly superior arms. The battle remained indecisive for several hours before the Indians finally withdrew, leaving a hundred prisioners and many dead behind them. They had, however, killed two Spaniards, if we may believe Mariño de Lobera's account obtained from soldiers who fought in the battle, and they also wounded a great many others as well as thirty horses.

This is the only battle in the whole of Almagro's campaign which is mentioned in any detail by Gongora Marmolejo. It provides eloquent testimony to the different mettle of the people to be found south of the Itata, and certainly did nothing to give any inducement to Almagro to reconsider his intention of withdrawing from this disappointing territory and returning to Peru.

Pedro de Valdivia himself, in his correspondence to Charles V, supplies further evidence. In the letter sent from La Serena on September 4, 1545, he states, "I have Francisco de Aguirre, my Captain . . . in the province of Itata, with a company of men at the *frontier line*, to keep the Indians of this province from crossing over to the other side." This is written in reference to the fact that the Spaniards required the more peaceable Indians of the territory north of the Itata for many menial services and were taking definite steps to prevent them from swelling the ranks of that strangely different fighting race which was holding out to the south of what even at this early stage begins to be described as a frontier.

Again, referring to his expedition south in 1546, he writes that he met with no difficulty until, after crossing the Itata, "we met with large hordes of warriors who came out to defend the paths against us." And later, in reference to these same warriors: "I have warred with men of many nations, but never have I seen such fighting tenacity as is displayed by these Indians." From a soldier of Pedro de Valdivia's ability and experience, this was high praise indeed. His reference is clearly to something very different from the Indians father north, who had already been put to work, in what amounted to a state of slavery, on the estates and in the mines of their new masters in the Mapacho and Aconcagua Valleys.

Miguel de Olivares when describing the *Huilliches,* or southern group of what we may describe as the older and more passive race, writes, "The Indians of Imperial and onwards are of the same quality as those around Santiago" (i.e., the *Picunches* north of the Itata) "and of little courage, and no stomach for fighting." Ovalle, also in reference to the *Huilliches,* describes them as "a peaceable people, of noble condition and very affectionate character, not warlike like the Araucanians, and in this opinion they are held and respected."

These extracts from the writings of observers at first hand provide sufficient indication of great differences of character, differences which are exceedingly difficult to explain among a single homogeneous race.

The arms employed by these peoples again show marked points of difference. Mariño de Lobera, describing the bows of the *Picunches,* writes, "extremely large bows are used for the shooting of arrows of great length and penetrating power, and such is the force of this weapon that the arrow will pass clean through a saddle tree and still continue its flight freely onwards." The Araucanian bows on the contrary were short, seldom a meter long, and dispatched an arrow of not more than half that length. Furthermore, the Araucanian arrow was tipped with a bone point, while *Picunches* and *Huilliches* both used stone arrowheads. The *Picunche* spears were from three to four meters long, or nearly twice the length of the Araucanian equivalent. The *Picunches* used clubs with stone or metal heads, and of relatively small dimensions, while the Araucanian club was a much larger affair, cut from a solid chunk of timber and generally slightly curved at its business end.

Finally there are the physiological differences between the two races, again by themselves almost conclusive in the opinion of those who have studied them. The following is taken from the first volume of Francisco Encina's *Historia de Chile*: "In their physical characteristics the differences between *Picunches* and *Huilliches* on the one hand, and genuine representatives of the pure *Mapuches* on the other, are strongly accentuated. Among the former predominated the subdolichocephalous or mesaticephalous type of skull, and the small head, the narrow relatively high forehead, and an occipital bone which was more protuberant than that displayed by the *Mapuche*. Of much the same height as the *Mapuche*, they were less corpulent, of a darker and more yellowish color, with less pronounced cheekbones, narrower faces, and larger noses, the latter frequently concave in shape. Their capillary system was more abundant, and their features in general displayed more regularity than those of the *Mapuches*."

Quite apart from this weight of evidence, there is the highly suggestive attitude of the Araucanians themselves towards their southern neighbors during the wars with the Spaniards. Though the Spanish governors formed two *Vutan-mapus*, or political divisions, for the purpose of dealing with the natives south of the river Toltén, the Araucanians refused to recognize their existence. The Spanish governors were compelled to receive the Araucanians on a different day from that on which audience was granted to the representatives of what the Araucanians regarded as inferior races.

Such is the outline of the case for ascribing an independent origin to the Araucanians. Opposed to it is the weight of Barros Arana's prestige and the one fact which in his view overbalanced all others, the common language which the Araucanians shared with *Picunches* and *Huilliches*. Latcham dismisses this difficulty by pointing out that the Araucanians were exogamous and married the women of the race they drove out. Since children tend to speak the language of their mothers, a few generations would be amply sufficient for the original Araucanian tongue to be completely lost. He cites the powerful example of children in Chile today, where the majority of those who bear foreign names, at all events in the second generation, know not one word of their grandfathers' tongues, nor in many cases can even pronounce those names in a manner which would be readily understood in the countries of their origin. In thus neatly disposing of this objection, Latcham failed to notice, or at all events to state, that he had thereby gone at least halfway toward agreement with Barros Arana. If the warriors who fought the Spaniards to a finish were descended from the males of a race of intruders, they no less certainly on this argument, carried in their veins the blood of *Picunche* and *Huilliche* matrons.

Whatever is the true story of the formation of the Araucanian race, one fact admits of no discussion. Their military qualities were unique. Never to the end did they display any lessening of the fighting courage which made them such formidable opponents. In battle the front ranks were ruthlessly sacrificed to the Spanish musketry in order that the succeeding ones might get to close quarters, but it was a place in the front rank which was most hotly competed for. Thayer Ojeda writes of the battle of Peteroa, the high water mark of Lautaro's fine and tragic attempt to rid his country of the Spaniards, "They fell one after another, covering the field of battle with their bodies, and their banners with glory. Deaf to offers of pardon, refusing to give or accept quarter, they died as heroes, Lautaro, eighteen captains, and 645 picked Araucanian fighting men."

As Francisco Encina points out, however, courage of this high quality, if misdirected, would have shortened rather than prolonged the struggle, and it is to the Araucanian head rather than to his heart that we must look to discover how he could fight on something approaching equal terms with his enemy. Diego de Almagro's expedition rode the first horses into Chile, and Reinoguelen was the Araucanians' first introduction to well-armed cavalry. Yet Pedro de Valdivia, describing his expedition of ten years later to the river Bío-Bío, reports that his horses could make no headway against the new tactics of the Indians there, and that he was forced to dismount and fight on foot when the animals began to refuse to face the enemy. Seventy horses were severely dealt with on this occasion. In 1555 the Araucanians had perfected the use of a special small club capable of stunning a horse with one blow. They used this with great effect when they defeated the Spaniards at Concepción in that year. At Marigueñu they tried out, with disastrous results for the Spaniards, a type of lasso consisting of a running noose fixed to a twelve-foot pole. After one man had thrown this over a horseman's head, several jumped to his aid in pulling the unfortunate Spaniard bodily from his mount. Nor was this all. They soon learned to use horses themselves, and turned them against their enemies with excellent effect. As early as November 30, 1557, Caupolican rode on a white charger at the battle of Millarapue, a horse which may have been Valdivia's own.

They quickly discarded the use of slings and arrows against armored enemies who were impervious to them. They concentrated on the use of pikes and the terrible *Macanas,* or heavy curved clubs, which they wielded with such devastating effect. They chose their battlegrounds near gullies and wooded slopes where horses would be at the greatest disadvantage. They learned to lead their enemy into difficult terrain, at the same time closing it behind him and blocking his line of retreat in a variety of ways. Above all they soon appreciated the futility of disorganized attacks in mass, hitherto their traditional method, and the value of a number of manageable units to be used as the tide of battle dictated. Gay writes in admiration, "Their tactics were those of Follard, or the Marshalls of Luxemburgh and Villars, and other authors of the art of warfare . . . Their adversaries were the conquerors of Europe . . . What the Spaniards were unable to accomplish, no army could have achieved in like circumstances."

From Tucapel onwards, the Spaniards became fully aware, as Pedro de Valdivia himself possibly never did, that they were fighting no common enemy. Curiously enough there is no bitterness in contemporary accounts. They are all, on the contrary, instinct with a tremedous admiration for these unusual foemen. Ercilla, who himself fought against them, wrote his epic *La Araucana* quite as much with the object of singing their praises as of giving a simple account of events which he had witnessed.

We will leave Francisco Encina, with his rare powers of penetration, to paint a picture of the Araucanian spirit. In a noteworthy passage, he quotes from Ercilla the lines describing the cruel punishment of the Araucanian chieftain Galvarino, when captured by the Spaniards. After the severance of his right hand, Galvarino gaily held forth the left for a fresh stroke of the executioner, in Ercilla's presence. "The fine sensibility of the poet," writes Encina, referring to Ercilla, "has captured the profound significance of the Indian's behavior, that virile pride which, incarnate in his gesture, rebukes with disdain the futile expedient calculated to intimidate his countrymen. Galvarino, once released, renews the struggle until once again he is made a prisoner, and Ercilla, who feels the temper of his soul, absents himself to avoid witnessing the iniquity of his execution. Nothing could be more opposed to the passive resignation before adversity which was displayed by the Peruvian Indians, and the greater part of those who populated the northern center and south of Chile."

It was not until 1883 that these unusual warriors finally laid down their arms for the last time, just 347 years after the Spaniards had first tasted their quality at Reinoguelen.

Notes

Chapter 1

1. The Spanish colonists in fact habitually referred to the Pacific as the South Sea (*Mar del Sur*) and the Atlantic as the North Sea (*Mar del Norte*). This was due to their relative positions as observed at the Isthmus of Panama.

2. J. Mujica de la Fuente, *Boletin de la Academia Chilena de la Historia*, 1936, p. 299.

Chapter 2

1. A *Castellano* was estimated as being worth three Chilean pesos and seven cents at a time when the Chilean peso was worth forty-eight English pence. The *Castellano* may be taken, therefore, as having a value of about twelve shillings, in terms of shillings as they were at the beginning of this century.

2. Mariño de Lobera, Ch. II.

3. Oviedo, Lib. XLVII, Cap. IV.

4. Herrera, Dec. VI, Lib. II, Cap. I.

5. *Ibid.*, Lib. III, Cap. IX.

6. *Ibid.*, Lib. III, Cap.X.

7. *Ibid.*, Lib. V, Cap. I.

8. Encina, Vol. I, p. 73.

Chapter 3

1. It will be noticed that Valdivia took his mother's and not his

father's name. Cunninghame Graham may be right in explaining it in the light of an old Spanish proverb: He who has a worthless father takes his mother's name (*El que tiene ruin padre, toma el nombre de la madre*).

2. Mariño de Lobera, Ch. XIV.

3. In his correspondence, Valdivia says the estate produced 200,000 *Castellanos* a year.

4. "*El Marqués me dixo que se espantaba como queria dexar lo que tenia, que era tan bien de comer como el.*" From Pedro de Valdivia's letter to his representatives at the Spanish Court dated October 15, 1550. The expression "*dar de comer*" (give to eat) was the one habitually used for the distribution of estates and native labor in newly conquered territory.

5. The acceptance of an appointment in another territory seems to have carried with it the automatic loss of property in the place where you were. Absentee landlords had no place in such unsettled outposts. If a man wanted land it was up to him to administer it and defend it.

6. "*Pizarro no me favoreció ni con un solo peso de la Caxa de S.M. ni suyo.*" From Valdivia's letter to his representatives at Court.

7. "*No habia hombre que quisiesse venir a esta tierra y los que mas huían de ella eran los que truxo el Adelantado don Diego de Almagro, que como lo desamparó, quedó tan mal infamada que como la pestilencia huían della.*" Valdivia's letter to Charles V dated September 4, 1545.

8. Commission from the Spanish Monarch dated January 24, 1539. See Medina's *Documentos Inéditos para la Historia de Chile,* Vol. VIII, p. 17.

9. Documentos Inéditos, Vol. VIII, p. 32.

10. La Grasca's letter to the Council of Indies dated November 26, 1548. See *Documentos Inéditos,* Vol. VIII, p. 248.

Chapter 4

1. Valdivia's letter of September 4, 1545, to Charles V.

2. Declaration of Bernal de Martin in the service record of Juan Gomez, dated November 20, 1558. See Vol. XIV, p. 24, *Documentos Inéditos.*

3. The conversation is recorded by Luis de Cartagena in testimony

given at Francisco de Villagra's trial. See Vol. XXII, p. 115, *Documentos Inéditos*.

4. At Villagra's trial. See Vol. XXII, p. 22, of *Documentos Inéditos*.

5. *Documentos Inéditos*, Vol. VIII, p. 32.

6. Valdivia's letter to Hernando Pizarro of September 4, 1545.

7. In the letter of September 4, 1545, to Charles V.

Chapter 5

1. *Historiadores de Chile*, Vol. I, p. 67

2. The following is quoted from Vol. II, p. 19, of Prescott's *Conquest of Peru* in regard to the foundation of Lima: "The name bestowed was . . . City of the Kings, in honor of the day, being the sixth of January, 1535, the festival of Epiphany, when it was said to have been founded, or more probably when its site was determined, *as its actual foundation seems to have been twelve days later*" (italics mine). We have not been able to discover that this is more than a coincidence. It is certainly a curious one.

3. Encina quotes these two extracts in Vol. I, pp. 193-195.

4. "Actas del *Cabildo* de Santiago," March 11, 1541.

Chapter 6

1. All the incidents and quotations leading up to Valdivia's acceptance of the title of Governor are, unless otherwise stated, taken from the Minutes of successive meetings of the Santiago Municipality ("Actas del Cabildo de Santiago") and may be found in the *Colección de Historiadores de Chile*, Vol. 1, pages 74 and following.

2. Mariño de Lobera, Ch. XIII.

3. "Actas del *Cabildo* de Santiago," June 10, 1541.

4. Mariño de Lobera, who supplies the greatest amount of detail regarding these events.

5. Mariño de Lobera, Ch. XIII.

Chapter 7

1. Mariño de Lobera, Ch. XV.

2. Mariño de Lobera, Ch. XV.

3. *Documentos Inéditos,* Vol. XIV, p. 478.

4. *Ibid.,* Vol. VIII, p. 53.

Chapter 8

1 *Documentos Inéditos,* Vol. VIII, p. 71.

2. *Ibid.,* p. 78.

3. Testimony of Hernan Rodriguez de Monroy at Valdivia's trial. See *Documentos Inéditos,* Vol. VIII, p. 315.

4. Valdivia's letter of September 4, 1545, to Charles V.

5. "Actas del *Cabildo* de Santiago," July 6, 1546.

6. *Documentos Inéditos,* Vol. XIV, p. 232.

7. Declarations of Alonso de Escobar, Gonzalo de los Rios, and Juan Gomez in the lawsuit brought by Juan Godinez against Esperanza de Rueda and Pedro de Miranda "concerning certain Indians." *Documentos Inéditos,* Vol. XIV, pp. 256, 265, and 274.

8. *Documentos Inéditos,* Vol. XIV, p. 250.

9. Declaration of Inés de Suarez at the trial of Francisco de Villagra. *Documentos Inéditos,* Vol. XXII, p. 625 and following.

10. Diego Fernandez, pp. 159-160.

Chapter 9

1. *Documentos Inéditos,* Vol. VIII, p. 319.

2. *Ibid.,* Vol. IX, p. 294.

3. Mariño de Lobera, Ch. XXV.

4. Statement of Juan Romero under examination. See *Documentos Inéditos,* Vol. VIII, p. 64.

5. *Documentos Inéditos,* Vol. VIII, p. 164.

6. *Ibid.,* p. 159.

7. *Ibid.,* p. 156.

8. *Ibid.,* p. 164.

9. *Ibid.,* Vol. XXII, pp. 239 and 586.

10. *Ibid.,* Vol XXI, p. 216.

11. *Ibid.,* Vol. VIII., p. 157.

12. *Ibid.,* Vol. XXII, p. 129.

13. *Ibid.,* p. 568.

Chapter 10

1. Diego Fernandez, Vol. I, p. 385.

2. Fernandez, *Historia del Peru,* Parte I, Lib. 2, Cap. 90.

3. This short conversation is recorded in Valdivia's letter of October 5, 1550, to Charles V.

4. La Gasca's letter of November 26, 1548 to the Council of Indies, reporting on Valdivia's trial. See *Documentos Inéditos,* Vol. III, p. 245.

5. La Gasca's letter of November 26, 1548, to the Council of Indies, reporting on Valdivia's trial. See *Documentos Inéditos,* Vol. VIII, pp. 247-248.

6. At the trial of Francisco de Villagra. See *Documentos Inéditos,* Vol. XXI, p. 475.

7. "Actos del *Cabildo* de Santiago," July 1, 1549.

Chapter 11

1. Gongora Marmolejo, Ch. X. The vivid wording shows evidence of his having taken part.

2. Valdivia's letter of October 15, 1550, to his Representatives at Court. Had it come from another source, one might have suspected at least some exaggeration. Coming from the source it does, it is incontestable.

3. Whereas the Santiago Municipality had resisted quite strongly the shortening of their Northern border from Copiapó to the river Choapa, the clearly implied shortening of their southern border from the river Itata to the river Maule seems to have provoked no reaction. Perhaps a growing feeling of Federal power was making them less sensitive to more local considerations. This must be conjectural, but the difference of attitude is striking.

4. On page 238 of his *Historia de la moneda Española* (Madrid, 1959), G. Farrés states that in 1566 a Maravedi was worth one-third of an English farthing of that date. The dictionary of Newman and Baretti (London, 1854), on page 269, states that a "Cuento is the product of 100,000 and 10" or, in other words, a million. On this basis, "Un Cuento de Maravedia" was worth approximately £347 in terms of the value of the English pound sterling in the middle of the sixteenth century.

5. *Documentos Inéditos,* Vol. IX, p. 115.

6. See Gongora Marmolejo, Ch. XII.

Chapter 13

1. This is the name which has been given to the civilization found in being among the central and southern Chilean natives (but excluding the Araucanians) at the time of the conquest. It is so called because it took its rise from the displacement southward of Peruvian tribes from the Chincha valley. See Ricardo Latcham's *Prehistoria Chilena.*

2. "It is certain that all his purpose and wish was to reach the Magellan Straits." Gongora Marmolejo, Ch. XIII.

Chapter 14

1. "Don Martin de Avendaño asked leave to go to Peru. Valdivia gave it gladly because he now despised everything. And dearly it was going to cost him." Gongora Marmolejo, Ch. XIV.

2. Gongora Marmolejo, Ch. XIV.

3. Statement of Antonio Diaz in proof of the service of Juan Jufré. See *Documentos Inéditos,* Vol. XIV, p. 106.

4. Statement of Guillermo Martin in proof of the services of Juan Jufré. See *Documentos Inéditos,* Vol. XIV, p. 44.

Chapter 15

1. Gongora Marmolejo, Ch. XIV.

2. *Ibid.*

3. *Admapu* was the Araucanian tribal law in all its extension.

4. There is no sure evidence of the date of Valdivia's birth, nor does he seem to have known it himself. As a witness to the services of Diego de Fuenmayor he gives testimony on October 2, 1537, and says that he is *"de edad de treinta y cinco años, poco mas o menos."* (*Documentos Inéditos,* Vol. V, p. 4.) This would make him approximately fifty-one or perhaps at most fifty-two when he died.

Bibliography

Amunategui, Domingo. *Las encomiendas de indigenas en Chile,* Santiago, 1909-10.

Amunategui, Miguel Luis. *Descubrimiento y conquista de Chile,* Santiago, 1862.

Barros Arana, Diego. *Historia General de Chile,* Santiago, 1884-1902.

Cabildo de Santiago, Actas del (*Colección de Historiadores de Chile,* Vol. I, Santiago, 1861)

Carvallo Goyeneche, Vincente. *Descripción historico-geografica del Reino de Chile* (*Colección de Historiadores de Chile,* Vols. IX and X), Santiago, 1875.

Cordoba y Figueroa, Pedro de. *Historia de Chile* (*Colección de Historiadores de Chile,* Vol. II), Santiago, 1862.

Cunninghame Graham, R.B. *Pedro de Valdivia, Conqueror of Chile,* London, 1926.

Encina, Francisco A. *Historia de Chile,* Santiago, 1940.

Ercilla y Zuñiga, Alonso de. *La Araucana,* Santiago, 1933.

Errazuriz, Crescente. *Historia de Chile. Pedro de Valdivia,* Santiago, 1911 and 1912.

Eyzaguirre, Jaime. *Ventura de Pedro de Valdivia,* Santiago, 1942.

Fernandez, Diego. *Historia del Peru,* Seville, 1571.

Fernandez de Oviedo y Valdés, Gonzalo. *Historia general y Natural de las Indias,* Madrid, 1855.

Gay, Claudio. *Historia fisica y politica de Chile,* Paris, 1884.

Garcilaso de la Vega (Inca). *Comentarios reales de los Incas, reyes que fueron del Peru,* Madrid, 1829.

Gongora Marmolejo, Alonso de. *Historia de Chile desde su descubrimiento hasta el ano 1575* (*Colección de Historiadores de Chile,* Vol. II), Santiago, 1862.

Herrera, Antonio de. *Historia general de los hechos de los Castellanos en las islas y tierra firme del mar océano,* Madrid, 1615.

Latcham, Ricardo. *La Prehistoria Chilena,* Santiago, 1928.

Mariño de Lobera, Pedro. *Cronica del Reino de Chile (Colección de Historiadores de Chile,* Vol. VI), Santiago, 1865.

Medina, Jose Toribio. *Colección de documentos inéditos para la historia de Chile,* Santiago, 1888-1902.

Molina, Cristobal de. *Relación de la conquista y población del Peru,* Lima, 1916.

Olivares, Miguel de. *Historia militar, civil, y sagrada de Chile (Colección de Historiadores de Chile),* Santiago, 1864.

Ovalle, Alonso de. *Historica relación del Reyno de Chile,* Santiago, 1888.

Rosales, Diego de. *Historia general del Reino de Chile,* Valparaiso, 1877.

Thayer Ojeda, Tomás. *Santiago durante el sigle XVI,* Santiago, 1905.

——*Los Conquistadores de Chile,* Santiago, 1908.

Valdivia, Pedro de. *Las cartas de Pedro de Valdivia,* Seville, 1929.

Vicuña Mackenna, Benjamin. *Historia de Santiago,* Santiago, 1869.

——*Las ultimas campañas de Pedro de Valdivia,* Santiago, 1884.

Index

INDEX

253

INDEX